რომ წაჰყვება საუკუნეს თქვენთან ჩემი ქნარი...

Through the ages, but with you, harp of mine will live...

აღმოაჩინეთ
გალაკტიონი

გალაკტიონ ტაბიძე: რჩეული ლექსები და მათი ახალი ინგლისური თარგმანი

ინგლისური თარგმანი ინესა მერაბიშვილისა

Critical, Cultural and Communications Press
London
2017

DISCOVER GALAKTION

GALAKTION TABIDZE: A SELECTION OF HIS POEMS IN A NEW PARALLEL TRANSLATION

Translated from Georgian by Innes Merabishvili

Critical, Cultural and Communications Press
London
2017

სარჩევი

CONTENTS

ლექსები

POEMS

ACKNOWLEDGEMENTS

The present book is a newly revised and enlarged edition of a bilingual volume of poems by Galaktion Tabidze (1891-1959) published by Critical, Cultural and Communications Press in 2011. Therefore, first and foremost, my thanks go to the publishers for their welcome attitude and readiness to popularise among English readers Georgia's greatest twentieth-century poet.

Early in the morning of 5 January 2004 I heard the doorbell ring. My visitor was Ms Nunu Ebanoidze, Galaktion Tabidze's step-daughter, who lived under the same roof as the poet for sixteen years, and who is one of the most knowledgeable students of his life. She bore in her arms a huge package, which, she said, was meant as a present for me in gratitude for my monograph *Galaktionic Enigmas.*[1] She opened the parcel and drew out a series of photographs of Galaktion Tabidze, a framed coloured portrait of her stepfather, which until that morning had hung over her bed, and a series of manuscripts, including a later version of the poem "Let Us Drink A Toast". The reader will understand the powerful emotions I felt. That very evening I decided to render Galaktion Tabidze's poems into English.

The winter vacation offered an ideal opportunity, and for many days and nights I was absorbed in my task. The publication of an essay[2] on the reaction to Lord Byron in Georgia gave me the opportunity to make renewed contact

---

[1] Innes Merabishvili, *Galaktionic Enigmas* (in the Georgian language with an English summary) (Tbilisi: The Georgian Byron Society, 2003).
[2] Innes Merabishvili, "Liberty and Freedom and the Georgian Byron", in *The Reception of Byron in Europe*, ed. Richard A. Cardwell (London-New York: Thoemmes Continuum, 2004), volume II, pp. 406-18.

with the editor Professor Richard A. Cardwell, and to ask him for an appraisal of my translations. Galaktion Tabidze was no stranger to the editor of the volume in which, following the tradition of Georgian thinkers, the poet was presented by me as the Georgian Byron.

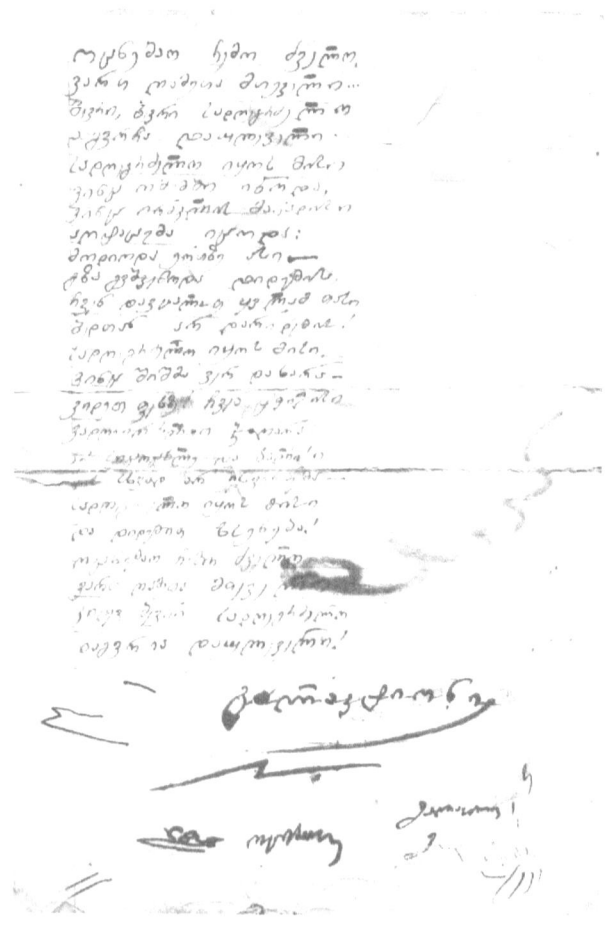

Autograph of the poem "Let us Drink a Toast" (1958)

From that new contact came a slim volume of Galaktion Tabidze's poems translated by me into English, edited by Professor Cardwell and published by Tbilisi University Press in 2005. I distributed that volume among my friends and colleagues when in England. It happened that one of the copies got into the hands of Lord Dominick Mereworth, a poet and a playwright, who enquired and managed to reach me in my home town by phone, though he had never met or heard of me before. Lord Mereworth expressed his high appreciation of the Georgian poet and developed an idea, very unexpected to me, to arrange an event in London in honour of Galaktion Tabidze. It was the outcome of his initiative that on 23 November 2011, Canning House in Belgrave Square, London, hosted a book launch of the earlier edition of the present work.

I express my most sincere gratitude to all the distinguished persons mentioned above. Cordial thanks also go to all those friends and colleagues who appreciated my translations of the Georgian poet and encouraged me to continue the work. Finally, I am happy to express special thanks to my family for their constant support in my Galaktionic endeavours.

Innes Merabishvili

Should I be sad or very proud,
When many flowers grow on the ground,
Exception is the fate of rose
To coexist with thorns and moans.

Innes Merabishvili

Galaktion's Life and Works

In the early spring of 1891, in a cottage belonging to the Tabidze family in the village of Chkvishi in Western Georgia, a young man lay dying of pneumonia. For over ten days and nights his wife was constantly at his bedside. He prayed that she would be strong because she had a duty to nurture and protect their only child, the baby son who lay asleep in the next room. His wife then revealed a secret to her husband: she was expecting another child. On hearing the news the dying man's face became radiant. He called for his father, asking him to bring a jug of wine. No one could refuse the wish of a dying man. They filled the glass with the wine and the man toasted the creature who was to be born in seven months time. He drained the glass to the dregs and breathed his last. On 17 November 1891 a boy was born to the widowed woman, whom she named Galaktion, or Galaxy. Several decades later Galaktion Tabidze would create a new galaxy of poetry.

At the outset of the twentieth century the modern poet faced the problem of giving expression to the upheavals caused by technical and political revolutions, especially the Russian Revolution. The distorted and convoluted images of the avant-garde became fashionable and accepted; poets and artists sought new symbols and fantastical images to express their heightened vision of their worlds. The French and European avant-garde – Expressionism, Cubism, Dada, Suprematism and Surrealism – took their places in the imaginations of Georgian artists, with the inevitable and complex changes required in style and expression.

Galaktion's birthplace, a cottage in Chkvishi.

Galaktion Tabidze was well read in world literature from the earliest times to the most recent European revolutionary expressions. Though he never became a follower of any of the contemporary movements, he had mastered the finest traditions of his native poetry. He gave new life to Georgian verse and established a new style in poetry that necessitated the creation of a new poetics and a new poetical form. Galaktion Tabidze's poetry is notable for musical verse based on inner melody, replete with novel images and vivid imagination. His poetry abounds in enigmatic metaphors and symbols. He created an incomparable realm of poetry as an inexhaustible source of depth, delight, purity and dramatic effect. Through his poems he expresses a strong belief that his poetry can transform the world. He once wrote:

> I have discovered a whole world,
> Unattainable for mankind yet.
>
> ("August Has Come")

Great art is always global, though it is always created in a certain country and in a certain environment. As for literature, its borders are more restricted as far as any literary text is of necessity enclosed within the limits of one language and, if not translated, is accessible only to the bearers of that tongue. Galaktion Tabidze nonetheless aimed to create poetry meant for the entire world. In one of his poems he expresses sorrow at the death of the great world thinkers of his epoch and ends the poem with the following stanza:

> I'm the only traveller that survived,
> To pass the fiery gales, yet never heard,
> To bring to Georgia sacred song of might,
> As a saviour, a saviour of the world.
>
> ("Prologue For 100 Poems")

In another poem the author compares himself to the Holy Grail:

> Sun of Ærraliða, sun of Ærraliða,
> Knelt down in prayer, I am as Holy Grail.
> Do spare the one whom I so dearly loved,
> Shelter her with your wings, I plead and pray.
>
> ("Sun Of Ærraliða")

Here, in all probability, the poet describes the purity of his feelings during prayer, on the one hand, but on the other, also the potentially inaccessible content of his poems, constantly inviting readers to reach an understanding, yet leaving much to be unveiled. The Holy Grail is something very valuable which is very hard to find. Different traditions describe it as a container or a stone with miraculous powers that provides happiness, eternal youth or sustenance in infinite abundance.

Galaktion with a group of students
at the Kutaisi Gymnasium, 1905.

The poet himself was considered by his contemporaries to be the "king of poets". He richly deserved this name as a result of the enormous popularity of his very first volumes of verses, *Poems*, published in 1914, and *Artistic Flowers in A Skull*, published in 1919. Alongside other Georgian poets like Besiki (Gabashvili), Ilya (Chavchavadze), Akaki (Tsereteli) or Vazha (Pshavela), Galaktion Tabidze is also widely known and affectionately called by his first name. Next to Rustvelology,[3] only Galaktion's poetry resulted in the establishment of a new field of Georgian philology, entitled Galaktionology.

When young, Galaktion lived mainly in Kutaisi, a major town in Western Georgia, a city famous for its cultural traditions. In 1917 he frequented Russia, mostly St Petersburg, but from 1918, following the Revolution, he established himself in Tbilisi, the capital of Georgia. In 1928 he travelled within the Soviet Union with a group of Georgian delegates to the Comintern, the Communist International Congress, and in 1935 visited Paris to participate in the Anti-Fascist Congress. He thus formed a part of the intellectual and artistic elite of the Soviet Communist State.

In 1912 Galaktion fell in love with Olga (Olya) Okujava, a young woman who shared his passion for poetry. Olga Okujava was from a family of Bolsheviks, though very educated. She herself was a strong believer in social changes through revolution. They married in 1916 but lived apart for long periods.

In spite of great revolutionary changes Galaktion was totally absorbed in his creative work. As the title of one of his poems says, it was poesy that proved to be his greatest aspiration: *Poesy, Poesy – First And Foremost!* During the February revolution in Russia, Galaktion happened to be back in Kutaisi, his home town. According to his journals, on one occasion he entered the theatre and found himself in a hall overcrowded by people who were shouting loudly:

---

[3] Shota Rustaveli, a great Georgian poet of the twelfth century, was the author of the Georgian national epic *Vepkhistkaosani* (*The Man in a Panther-Skin*), which draws on ancient Greek and Eastern philosophy in the celebration of heroism, love and friendship.

"Revolution! Revolution! Banners!" Some of them recognized the poet, lifted him up on their shoulders and carried him along the hall with the same shouts. Galaktion was deeply touched by such a welcome and the call for freedom that filled the atmosphere. As a result of those emotions he composed a poem, "Keep Banners High!". Since then this has been a very famous and beloved piece of poetry in Georgia as an appeal for Freedom and Liberty.

Kutaisi at the beginning of twentieth century.

The end of twenties was famous for a new wave of political contradictions in the Soviet Union. Many old Bolsheviks were suspected of being unfaithful to revolutionary ideas. Olga Okujava's family also fell under scrutiny, and in 1929 she was arrested and sent into exile to Uzbekistan. Times were difficult and dangerous in Soviet Georgia during the period of the Stalinist political purges. Donald Rayfield has noted that "by luck or cunning [Galaktion] avoided groups, even friendships, and was spared the political manoeuvres and purges of the Georgian Union of

Writers in the 1930s".[4] Of course that is true. Galaktion tried to survive:

> If I could but survive this winter,
> If winds could spare me and leave!

("Snow")

Olga Okujava

A rumour rose in Tbilisi that it was Stalin, the Soviet leader of Georgian origin, who spared Galaktion with the invisible hand. It is said that when a delegation of Georgian writers was to arrive in Kremlin to meet the Soviet leader, the list of delegates was sent beforehand to Moscow. Apparently under the influence of enemies, the poet was not included

---

[4] Donald Rayfield, *The Literature of Georgia: A History* (London: Routledge, 2000), p. 253.

in that group. When Stalin saw the list of writers submitted by the Georgian Government, he enquired on the spot: "Where is the King of Poets?"

Galaktion when awarded the Order of Lenin

Soviet workers and representatives of intelligentsia were strongly advised to join the Communist Party and serve it faithfully. At the same time membership was especially favourable for their future career and promotion. In spite of the fact that Galaktion never expressed his willingness and never became the member of the Communist Party, in 1932 he was awarded the Order of Lenin, the highest award for very honourable Soviet people.

To please the poet, the Soviet Government released Olga Okujava and she returned to Georgia. To enjoy the reunion the couple went for a holiday to Kobuleti, a resort on the coast of the Black Sea. Unfortunately, several years later she was blamed for being a follower of Trotsky's ideas and was again arrested. At first she was kept in prison in Tbilisi but, in 1936, as a victim of the Stalinist purges, she was sent into exile to Russia without permission to correspond. It happened that Olya's letters reached Galaktion. The letters show that she never received a response to them, though she pleaded him to drop a line. Some biographers assume that Galaktion never replied to her out of fear of being compromised. But had Galaktion answered his wife, his letters would have been destroyed in transit. Sources show that Galaktion attempted to correspond with her through a trustworthy friend, who wrote in her name and handwriting, but in vain. The strain led Galaktion to alcoholism and depression. It is obvious that Olga Okujava was predestined for a severe punishment. In 1941 she was executed in Oryol, Russia, far away from Georgia. A mystical poem, "Her Eyes Stayed Open As She Died" creates the impression that Galaktion anticipated her death:

> She died with somewhat helpless death,
> It was a strange and feeble death!
> Her eyes stayed open! Oh, her eyes!
> Her eyes stayed open as she died.
> She died afar in foreign lands,
> With eyes still open lay she dead!

In 1943 Galaktion met and married Nino Kvirikadze, whom he had admired in his youth, the widow of David Ebanoidze, a military engineer, also the victim of those purges. Neither marriage produced children but Galaktion happily adopted Nino's son and daughter by her previous marriage. Galaktion and Nino lived together until the poet's death.

In spite of the enormous affection shown him by his fellow countrymen he was never easy or content with the company of his fellow writers, especially those favoured by the Soviet hierarchy and official cultural circles. Poetic lines reveal his objections towards them:

Galaktion with his second wife, Nino Kvirikadze, and his
stepdaughter, Nunu Ebanoidze, Sukhumi, 1946

Let now the windbags hear me well:
When weathered I in winds like hell,
On meadows with nightingales sweet,
You, poets of Georgia, were asleep.

("You Wouldn't")

Some proud communists of those times used to heap
reproaches on the poet for his not joining the Communist
Party. Galaktion answered them with challenging humour:
"The certificate of your being the member is in your
pocket, but mine is over my breast." But there were
occasions when, deliberately or due to carelessness,
Galaktion after drinking left his Order of Lenin in a pub.
His devoted fans would keep it safe until his return back or

deliver it to him at home. The news spread very quickly and reached one of the Secretaries of the Central Committee, who invited Galaktion to his office to discuss the case, which could have led to some kind of punishment.

"Your senior comrade is very annoyed," said the Secretary, meaning the First Secretary at the time.

"Whom do you mean by my senior comrade?" corrected the poet. "The only senior comrade of mine is Akaki Tsereteli."[5] With that he patted the leader on the cheek with his gloved hand, as if to humour him. That was the way he left. Only Galaktion could permit himself such an answer and such a liberty.

[5] Akaki Tsereteli, a great Georgian poet of the nineteenth century, who especially inspired Galaktion.

Shortly before his death, in 1959, Galaktion agreed to sit
for his portrait by a young artist Nelly Kandelaki

Galaktion felt the affection of the nation towards him and enjoyed very much public readings of his poems. People recognized him in the streets and never missed a chance to express their love and appreciation towards him. He was a real living king of poetry.

Galaktion at the Decade of Georgian Arts and Literature in Moscow, 1958

Gentle and cheerful in private life, he was a lonely man who endured deep and tragic suffering. His natural depressive temperament drove him to attempt suicide on several occasions, but he was saved at the last minute by occasional eyewitnesses. "Dying", wrote Sylvia Plath prophetically before committing suicide herself, "is an art, like everything else, / I do it exceptionally well. / I do it so it feels like hell" ("Lady Lazarus"). Galaktion finally did it well on 17 March 1959 by throwing himself from the upper floor of the hospital in which he had been interned for treatment for depression.

At the age of 28 Galaktion wrote:

> But if my country fails to treat me well,
> Yes! I'll die a death, a poet's name deserves.
> ("Poesy, Poesy – First And Foremost!")

The nation went into deep mourning and he was buried with state honours in the Pantheon of Poets and Writers on Mtatsminda (Holy Mountain), in Tbilisi. His *Collected Works* were published in twelve volumes by the leading Georgian publishing house Sabchota Sakatrvelo between 1966 and 1975. Twenty five volumes of his writings taken from manuscript sources and his extant archive were published in Tbilisi several years ago.

Galaktionic Enigmas

Sadly Galaktion's poetry is almost unknown to the outside world for two main reasons: the limited number of Georgians abroad on the one hand and, on the other, the fact that his verses are virtually untranslatable owing to the abundance of unusual and enigmatic expressions so common, for example, in avant-garde writing. As has been noted above, Galaktion never followed any contemporary movements but created a new poetics.

Though his enigmatic expressions resist easy analysis and many of his unusual word combinations, images and symbols remained unexplained even by Georgian scholars, his poetry has always caused infectious emotions and has found a ready response among his readers, but not translators. I had good fortune to develop a meticulous study of Galaktion's poetry from the point of view of modern linguistics, especially stylistics, semasiology and text linguistics, but also based on my experience of dealing with poetic texts for many decades. As a result I produced two monographs[6] dedicated to the unveiling of his enigmas, and these actually led me to render Galaktion into English.

Even in Galaktion's lifetime and after, with very rare exceptions, there developed an opinion that his poetry was untranslatable. Galaktion himself strongly objected to this point of view and kindly encouraged translators to render his poetry into foreign languages. As Paulo Rônai[7] points out in his *School of Translators*, the aim of all art is something impossible when the painter reproduces the irreproducible, the poet expresses the inexpressible and the translator strives to translate the untranslatable. There is no doubt that Galaktion managed to express the inexpressible. Therefore, we aimed to translate the untranslatable. But what is untranslatable in Galaktion's poetry and how can we render it?

Translation of poetry as well as of any literary text involves at least two necessary stages, textual interpretation and its artistic realisation in a different language. A skilled reader can feel and understand poetry without the need to be versed in stylistic and linguistic methods. However, by making use of a modern linguistic approach, analysis of Galaktion's enigmatic lines and translation of them becomes possible. Though the present volume offers to the English readers only sixty poems from Galaktion's *oeuvre*, it may be useful to offer a short analysis of some of his enigmatic lines, especially with the aim of understanding

---

[6] Innes Merabishvili, *Galaktionic Enigmas* (see footnote 1 above); Innes Merabishvili, *Galaktion's Mary – in search of a prototype*, in the Georgian language with an English summary, (Tbilisi: The Georgian Byron Society, 2012).
[7] Haroldo de Campos, "On Translation as Creation and Criticism", in *Haroldo de Campos in Conversation*, ed. by Bernard McGuirk and Else R. P. Vieira (London: Zoilus Press, 2009), p. 200.

his way of visualising the world through unusual icons and their uncommon correlations.

For example, the componential method of analysis offers to split the meaning of a word into semas as minimal units of meaning.[8] Thus, the meaning of a word is presented as consisting of different semas when each of them has its own definite weight on the plane of content. Semas of maximum weight create the kernel of the meaning. The other semas are of less weight and surround the kernel as secondary features. In poetic texts, especially in unusual word combinations, we can deconstruct the meaning into different semas, where under the influence of context they are newly arranged. Therefore, a new kernel and new secondary semas are formed and their combination creates a new contextual meaning in a chain of signifiers.

Take, for example the line "The soul wept out with light blue wines" from a poem of the same title. The most unusual point about this line is the word combination "light blue wines" in so far as wine is normally used to imply either a dark red colour or the light colour of grapes, but never blue or light blue. The leading lexical sema of the noun "wine" is "an alcoholic drink made from grapes or other fruits". Next to the leading sema we distinguished other semas, such as "getting drunk", "frank", "brave", "lacking precaution", "illogical", "elated", etc., to say nothing of the semas of colour. On the other hand, the adjective "light blue" comprises such semas as "resembling heaven", "heavenly", "unearthly", "pure", "clear", and so on. All the above-mentioned semas of "light blue" might be attributed to fit the secondary lexical semas of the noun "wine", thus converting the direct meaning of the word into the

---

[8] Innes Merabishvili, *A Linguistic Image and a New Semantic Triangle*, in: *US-China Foreign Language*, David Publishing Company, New York, Volume 15, Number 6, June, 2017, p. 367-374.

figurative meaning of "high spiritual condition". Therefore, the combination of "soul" with "light blue wines" through the verb "to weep" seems apt, especially from the point of view of poetical vision.

Besides, as a linguist, I argue that, together with sound, form and concept that give a word its meaning, any lexical unit comprises an image reflected from a class of objects of extralinguistic reality that it denotes.[9] In ordinary speech image is not active, but in artistic speech, as if called forth by the user of the word, it becomes the leader of the word meaning. Galaktion reasons through images or icons enclosed in words, and this is his great novelty. Therefore, when translating Galaktion we need to retain images offered by him as freshly and impressively as possible, while remaining "true" to the original text. That is how "the soul wept out with light blue wines", or why the poet is "fond of flakes of violet snow like virgins falling from a bridge" ("Snow").

Apart from the inner structure of the word, symbols in Galaktion's poetry are of special importance. The word "rose" serves as a good example. More myth and legend surrounds the rose than any other flower. Throughout history this flower has conjured up passion, tenderness, victory, pride, fidelity, death, and the quest for love. The symbolism of a rose is completed by its thorns, sharp reminders of the pain that flows from love. Besides, the rose has served as a Christian religious symbol for centuries and is commonly associated with the Virgin Mary. Madonnas are frequently painted crowned with roses. Roses are linked through the Virgin Mary to Christian purity. The Virgin Mary is called a "rose without thorns", because of the tradition that she was free from the stain of original sin. In Galaktion's poems a rose displays several of its symbolic meanings simultaneously. The following

---

[9] *Ibid.*

poems could serve as confirmation: "Aspen Trees", "Evening", "The Moon Of Mtatsminda", "An Angel Was Holding A Long Parchment", "Azure-Land As Rose In Sand", "The Soul Wept Out With Light Blue Wines".

The Virgin Mary
Virgin of the Gate, Iveron, Mount Athos

In the poem "The Moon of Mtatsminda" we read:

> An old man's ghost, so close to me, is in royal sleep,
> And the cemetery's filled with a sorrow deep,
> With a daisy and a rose under merry stars...
> Oh, these sites are haunted oft by the lonely bard...

Alongside distinct symbolic meanings such as that of beauty, love, death, etc., "a rose" here carries the suggestion of the Virgin Mary, especially when daisies are used next to it as a symbol of the innocence of the Christ Child. Towards the end of the fifteenth century the daisy came to be used in paintings of the Adoration as a symbol of the innocence of the Christ child. Apparently, the sweet simplicity of the daisy was felt to be a better symbol of His innocence than the tall, stately lily.[10]

In another example the symbolic meaning of roses and daisies, used in pairs, is accomplished by the symbolism of aspen trees:

> When from the mounts the cold wind blows,
> When mist is spreading like a sail,
> An army of white aspen leaves
> May rustle as a fairy tale.
> This ancient tale makes thrilled and drunk,
> And I am drunk with oldest wines,
> In recollections then I grasp
> The roses, daisies that were mine.
>
> ("Aspen Trees")

There are two early legends about the aspen tree. One relates that the cross, on which Jesus was crucified, was made from the aspen, and that, when the tree realised the

---

[10] George Ferguson, *Signs and Symbols in Christian Art* (Oxford: Oxford University Press, 1971), p. 30.

purpose for which it was being used, its leaves began to tremble with horror and have never ceased. The other legend is that, when Christ died on the cross, all the trees bowed in sorrow except the aspen. Because of its pride and sinful arrogance the leaves of the aspen were doomed to continual trembling.[11] That is how aspen trees also tremble in Galaktion's other poems:

> I stood in grief and did not quit,
> In front of me stood aspen trees,
> Black, rustling with dark-sounded leaves
> As if a soaring eagle's wings.

("Mary")

That is how layers of meanings accumulate and polyphony of content is created by Galaktion.

Besides the plane of content there is a plane of form and sound that actually creates music and invites the reader, though it offers a hard task for any translator. Concerning the sounds in Galaktion, we could offer an example, where consonants and vowels sound through alliteration. When translating Galaktion's famous poem "Whirls The Wind" ("Kari Hkris"), in which "kari" means "the wind" and "hkris" as a verb is translated into English as "blows" or "whirls", I prefer to choose the verb "whirl" because, together with the noun "wind", it helps to reproduce alliteration through the sound [w] in both English words corresponding to the alliteration of [kr] in the Georgian word combination ['kʌrɪ 'hkris]. At the same time I retain the number of syllables in each line to transform the metre and rhythm of the Georgian verse.

['kʌrɪ 'hkris, 'kʌrɪ 'hkris, 'kʌrɪ 'hkris]
Whirls the wind, whirls the wind, whirls the wind.

---

[11] *Ibid.*, p. 28.

One of Galaktion's literary characters, Mary, as an evoked image of remote and unshared love, is an exceptional favourite. She emerges in a number of his lyrical poems and some are specifically dedicated to her. The most beautiful and popular among them is the poem "Mary". Since its publication Georgian readers have connected the poem with a famous beauty, Mary Shervashidze, the poet's contemporary. However, it is a known fact that Galaktion never met her, although he might have imagined her, or noticed her in Kutaisi, where she lived for a period. As studies reveal, in Galaktion's poetry the word "Mary" acquires at least two meanings: it the name of a beloved lady, a symbol of lost love and constant sorrow, and the name of the Virgin Mary, as a symbol of divine love, eternal purity and Christian devotion. With regard to the first image, it is more than likely that Mary as a symbol of lost love must have derived from Byron, largely because of the prominence of Byron's Mary in Russian poetry (principally in Pushkin, Lermontov and Blok). One of Galaktion's lyrics dedicated to Mary under the title "With Mary's Eyes" is clearly a free translation of Byron's "Hills Of Annesley" (the 1805 fragment). But this instance is neither a case of a simple influence nor mere imitation, in that Galaktion goes far beyond his source when he develops Byron's vision and creates his own "Queen of a Fantastic Realm". The plot of "Mary" can be associated with the marriage of Miss Mary Chaworth, Lord Byron's early unshared love. In the untitled poem "The Two Great Seas Have Met Each Other", Galaktion mentions Byron together with Mary Chaworth. The first version of this poem was inscribed by Galaktion on the back of a postcard, showing Lord Byron in a boat in the company of Shelley, Mary Godwin, Claire Clairmont, Dr Polidori and others. The Georgian name for the Holy Virgin is "Mariam", and not "Mary", but both are female names in Georgia. Galaktion was the first to introduce Mary as a literary character in Georgian literature and to connect it with the Virgin Mary. Thus, we may argue that, alongside the European literary image of Mary, and especially that created by Lord Byron, the Georgian poet, alongside the name of a beloved lady, alludes to another English usage of "Mary", the name of the Blessed Virgin, thus referring to the symbolic meaning of a rose as well.

A postcard, showing Byron in a boat in the company of Shelley, Mary Godwin, Claire Clairmont, Dr Polidori and others

Galaktion frequently speaks of Byron in his letters and often alludes to him in his poems. Galaktion translated various short fragments from Byron's "Ode To Napoleon Buonaparte", "Darkness", and "The Deformed Transformed", though he translated Byron's lines into Georgian from Russian. English was not spoken then in Georgia and Galaktion did not know the language. Following the existing traditions he learned French and knew Russian perfectly well. Therefore, he read Byron in Russian and was greatly moved not only by Byron's poetic achievements, but also by his personality. Byron's lyricism and expressed sorrow were especially close to Galaktion's own poetic vision. Many aspects of Galaktion's poetic vision inspired his colleagues and friends to give him the name of the "Georgian Byron" (kartveli baironi).

In Galaktion's poetry, alongside the established symbolic content, a word may acquire a new meaning such as that based on the poet's individual vision. Together with references to beauty, love, death, etc., Galaktion develops for "a rose" the meaning of a masterpiece as the crown of one's reasoning and thinking, the pinnacle of creative activities. This meaning of "a rose" appears clearly realised in the poem "Roses", composed in 1927. Alluding to Hellas, Hesiod, Homer, Ovid, Botticelli and Raphael, Galaktion speaks of their roses as masterpieces. Salvador Dali's painting *A Meditative Rose* (1958) is a nice example of coincidence in the way of great artists' reasoning.

In a short poem, "Is Life Too Hard For You, My Heart?", composed in 1927 when the poet was thirty-six, he expresses willingness to bring to fame autumnal flowers, i.e. the fruits of his creative work, especially when we know that Galaktion published his second volume of poetry in 1919 under the title *Artistic Flowers In A Skull*. The poet is sorry not to find roses among those flowers: "No roses ever are around". It is obvious that by "roses" Galaktion means his masterpieces created much earlier, such as "The Night And I", "Mountains Of Guria", "Without Love", "Aspen Trees", "Evening", "The Moon of Mtatsminda", "Mary", "Snow", "Sun Of Ærraliða", and others.

As has been noted above, Galaktion's poetry is distinguished for musical verse based on inner melody. It is a well known fact that Galaktion, who was knowledgeable in music, was also very sensitive to it:

As if all spreading fair roses
The soul was full of Heaven's spell,

Contained much of Chopin's music
And Paganini's fancy realm.
> ("The Soul Wept Out With Light Blue Wines")

It is not easy to compose music for Galaktion's lines, which are endowed with unique and refined music of their own. In spite of this, Georgian composers have been creating songs for his verses with great enthusiasm, but the winner in success and popularity is the music based on the short poem "Is Life Too Hard For You, My Heart?" composed by Bidzina Kvernadze for Giga Lortkipanidze's TV serial *Data Tutashkhia* (1978). My translated version of this poem is intended to fit the melody of the famous Georgian song, the scores of which are enclosed in the present volume, following the Translator's Notes.

But as Galaktion's other lines claim, the dearest masterpiece, ever created and to be created, is his homeland:

> სადღაც რეკავს დაირა
> და სიცილის წვეთება,
> საქართველო! – აი რა
> არის შემოქმედება.
>
> ("კოსმიური რკესტრი")

With sounds of ringing laughter drops
Somewhere jingles a tambourine,
What is creation? – First of all,
My native Georgia – Land of green!
> ("Cosmic Orchestra")

Innes Merabishvili

41

ლექსები

POEMS

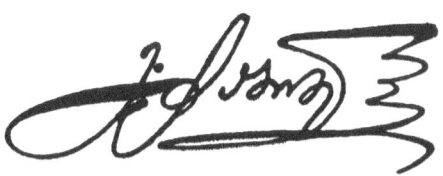

რაც უფრო შორს ხარ

რაც უფრო შორს ხარ, მით უფრო გტკები!
მე შენში მიყვარს ოცნება ჩემი,
ხელუხლებელი – როგორც მზის სხივი,
მიუწვდომელი – როგორც ედემი.

და თუ არა ხარ ის, ვისაც გფიქრობ,
მე დღეს არ გნადველობ, დაე, ვცდებოდე!
ავადმყოფ გულს სურს, რომ მას ოცნების
თეთრ ანგელოზად ევლინებოდე.

დაიწვას გული უცნაურ ტრფობით,
ცრემლით აივსოს ზღვა-საწყაული,
ოღონდ მჯეროდეს მე ჩემი ბოდვა
და სიყვარულის დღესასწაული.

1908

THE MORE AWAY

The more away, the more I love!
In you I love my dearest dream,
It feels – as if in Eden lives,
Untouched – as if the sun's bright beam.

You differ, maybe, from that dream,
I never grieve about it now!
My aching heart is apt to wish
You were an angel white endowed.

Let ardour strange all burn my heart,
Let seas be filled with tears I shed,
To trust the miracle of Love,
And ravings of a lover mad.

მე და ღამე

ეხლა, როცა ამ სტრიქონს ვწერ, შუადამე
    იწვის, დნება,
სიო, სარკმლით მონაქროლი, ველთა
    ზღაპარს მეუბნება.

მთვარით ნაფენს არემარე ვერ იცილებს
    ვერცხლის საბანს,
სიო არხევს და ატოკებს ჩემს სარკმლის წინ
    იასამანს.

ცა მტრედისფერ, ლურჯ სვეტებით ისე არის
    დასერილი,
ისე არის საფსე გრძნობით, ვით რითმებით ეს
    წერილი.

საიდუმლო შუქით არე ისე არის
    შესუდრული,
ისე საფსე უხვ გრძნობებით, ვით ამ ღამეს
    ჩემი გული.

დიდი ხნიდან საიდუმლოს მეც ღრმად გულში
    დავატარებ,
არ ვუმჟდავნებ ქვეყნად არვის, ნიავსაც კი არ
    ვაკარებ.

რა იციან მეგობრებმა, თუ რა ნაღველს
    იტევს გული,
ან რა არის მის სიღრმეში საუკუნოდ
    შენახული.

THE NIGHT AND I

At composing these true lines the midnight's melting,
    burning down,
The wind is whiffling through skylights calling tales
    from distant mounts.

The moon has spread a silver blanket, the ambience is
    all snow white,
Lilacs play and toss in bows near my casement,
    breezing light.

As with gentle secret caution, the sky is slashed with
    grey-blue stripes,
Filled they are with magic motion, like the rhymes
    amid these lines.

None is seen and none is spoken, night is mystery
    indeed,
The air is filled with deep emotions, like my heart full
    to the brim.

And this heart a secret treasures long-time now and
    since the past,
I do cosset it, do cherish, to a man will never trust.

Oh, my friends will never know the grief I suffered,
    pains I felt,
For this sorrow as a vow in my heart is deeply kept.

ვერ მომპარავს ბნელ გულის ფიქრს წუთი
    წუთზე უამესი,
საიდუმლოს ვერ მომჰტაცებს ქალის ხვევნა
    და ალერსი;

ვერც ჟილის დროს ნელი ოხვრა, და ვერც
    თასი ღვინით სავსე,
ვერ წამართმევს მას, რაც გულის ბნელ
    სიღრმეში მოვათავსე.

მხოლოდ ღამემ, უძილობის დროს სარკმელში
    მოკამკამემ,
იცის ჩემი საიდუმლო, ყველა იცის თეთრმა
    ღამემ.

იცის – როგორ დავრჩი ობლად, როგორ
    ვევნე და ვეწამე,
ჩვენ ორნი ვართ ქვეყანაზე: მე და ღამე, მე
    და ღამე!

1913

No embraces and no kisses, no sweet lips of damsels
   fair,
No, no one can ever steal the darkened thoughts of
   lonely care.

Nor the sighs I heave at night, nor the wine bowls full
   to the brim,
Can deprive me of recesses in the heart of hearts I
   keep.

But the night at sleepless times, as penetrating through
   skylights,
Learned and shared all the stories, all the secrets of my
   life.

Knows – how I became an orphan, knows my tortures,
   knows my blights,
In the world we're together: the Night and I, the Night
   and I.

ბურიის მთები

წინ, მეეტლევ!
ეგ ცხენები გააქანე, გააქანე!
მსურს, რომ ერთხელ კიდევ ვნახო
    გაზაფხულის მთები მწვანე,
მსურს, რომ დაფნით გადავზხლართოთ მძიმე
    ფიქრთა
ოკეანე!..
წამიყვანე!
მთები! როგორ შვენით მათზე გაზაფხულის
    ბუჩქ-ფოთოლი.
როგორ შვენის ველზე ნამი, გამჭვირვალე,
    როგორც ბროლი,
ცა ისეა მოწმენდილი, ცა ისეა შეუმკრთალი,
რომ ანგელოზს დაინახავს მოდარაჯე კაცის
    თვალი.
კიპარისი ისე დელავს, ისე დელავს, ისე
    დელავს,
ისე ტოკავს, ისე ტოკავს, როცა ქარი
    გადათელავს...
წყარო, კლდეში მოჩუხჩუხე, წვეთანკარა, ვით
    ცის ვნება,
დაფნის ბუჩქთა მწვანე ჩარჩოს ეომება,
    ეხეოქება.
და ჩანჩქერი მთით ნასხლეტი, დაფერილი
    დილის სხივით,
ძირს ემუხება და იფრქვევა და გადადის რძის
    ქაფივით.
ვდგევარ მთაზე... და სიჩუმის იდუმალი
    მესმის ენა,

MOUNTAINS OF GURIA[1]

Forward! Forward, cabman!
Drive the horses forth!
I would twine with laurels oceans of my thoughts!..
Bring me to the mountains into clouds that rear,
Dart me forward, cabman!
Dart away from here!
Spring has clothed the mountains in a dress of green,
Crystal dews are sparkling over the grass in fields!
The sky is now so clear, as has never been found,
Watching eyes may notice angels with the clouds.
Waves the wild cypress, waves now, oh, how it waves,
Throbs it, throbs it, throbs it, winds when overweigh.
A welling spring there bubbles, pure as heaven's love,
Rushing from rocks down, beating laurel shrubs.
Waterfall is jumping over crags, steep slopes,
Lit by morning sunbeams, splashing milky foam.
I'm on the mountain top, to the silence hark,

და მიტაცებს სწრაფი ფრთებით პოეტური
აღმაფრენა.
ვხედავ სურებს, ვხედავ დაფნარს, ვხედავ
მდუმარ ნასაკირალს,
ვხედავ სოფლებს სიცოცხლისას, განახლების
თვალით მზირალს.
ჩუმად! ვიდაც მდერის მთაზე... რა ძალაა ამ
ტკბილ ხმაში!..
არსად ისე არ მდერიან, როგორც აქ, ამ
ქვეყანაში,
არსად, არსად არ არსებობს ბრძოლის ჟინი,
ბრძოლის ქარი,
არსად ისე არ გადმოხეთქს უკმარობის
ნიაღვარი,
და არსად მთელ ქვეყანაზე არ ჰკოცნიან ისე
ვნებით,
ისე ცეცხლით, ისე ჟინით და იმგვარი
გატაცებით,
ვერსად ისე ვერვინ გაგხვევს გამოუცნობ
ცეცხლის ტბაში,
როგორც ლერწამქალწულები − აქ, ამ
წარმტაც ქვეყანაში!
და, მეეტლევ,
თუ მათ ალერსს ვერ ვედირსე, გეთაყვანე,
საალერსოდ ისევ მიწვევს გაზაფხულის
მთები მწვანე...
მაშ, გარეკე ებ ცხენები,
სადმე შორს, შორს წაიყვანე,
გამაქანე,
გამაქანე!

1914

As if floating with the wind, an inspired bard.
Here are hills, mute white cliffs,[2] fields that are so
    vast,
Living vills, with aims new, winning o'er the past.
Oh, be silent, silent! A song's heard from mounts,
What great power and what strength is in these sweet
    sounds!..
In no other countries, in no other climes
Singing moves and thrills you, as in land of mine.
Here the will to fight is of special sense,
Never in obedience – that's what others learn.
Here the lovers' kisses are fiery and with zest,
In no lands and climes, oh, kisses are so blessed.
Being in love is magic with our damsels fair,
No, nowhere you find for them a true compare!
If I fail to gain their love and their fond'st care,
Cabman, dear, this is all that I say and dare,
The spring mounts'll call me forth to caress with
    flare...
Drive the horses, drive them forth,
Forward them somewhere!
Dart me, dart me,
Dart me, forth!

უსიყვარულოდ

უსიყვარულოდ...
მზე არ სუფევს ცის კამარაზე,
სიო არ დაჰქრის, ტყე არ კრთება
სასიხარულოდ...
უსიყვარულოდ არ არსებობს
არც სილამაზე,
არც უკვდავება არ არსებობს უსიყვარულოდ.
მაგრამ სულ სხვაა სიყვარული
უკანასკნელი,
როგორც ყვავილი შემოდგომის
ხშირად პირველს სჯობს,
იგი არ უხმობს ქარიშხლიან
უმიზნო ვნებებს,
არც ყმაწვილურ ჟინს, არც ველურ ხმებს
იგი არ უხმობს...
და შემოდგომის სიცივეში
ველად გაზრდილი,
ის გაზაფხულის ნაზ ყვავილებს
სულაც არა ჰგავს...
სიოს მაგივრად ქარიშხალი
ეალერსება
და ვნების ნაცვლად უხმო ალერსს
გარემოუცავს.
და ჯანება, ჯანება სიყვარული
უკანასკნელი,
ჯანება მწუხარედ, ნაზად, მაგრამ
უსიხარულოდ.

WITHOUT LOVE

Without love
There lives no sun high in the Heavens,
Breeze never blows, no woods quiver
To please the one...
Without love there never exists
Any beauty,
No immortality ever lives
Without love.
But the last love is different,
All different,
Like an autumn flower oft better than
The love
That is first and yields to aimless passions,
Youthful whims,
Tireless and fervent, known for wild darts...
In valleys,
In autumnal coldness it's grown,
And is never like a spring flower,
Gentle and smart...
Is never caressed by breeze, but by
Whirling winds,
Instead of desire by voiceless endearment calmed.
And thus, the last love is being withered,
Being withered,
Full of sorrow, though tender, but joyless
And glum.

და არ არსებობს ქვეყანაზე
თვით უკვდავება,
თვით უკვდავება არ არსებობს
უსიყვარულოდ!

1914

No immortality ever lives
In the world,
No immortality ever lives
Without love!

მერის თვალებით

ეს რამდენიმე დღეა და რამდენიმე ღამე
დახურულია გული, როგორც საკანი რამე.
თითქო უმძიმეს კარებს კუპრის დაედო ლუქი,
გულში ვერც ზეცა ატანს, ვერც სიხარულის
    შუქი.
გაუდაბურდა ჩემი ყოფნის ყოველი წამი,
ეს რამდენიმე დღეა და რამდენიმე ღამე.
ოჰ, მომეცალეთ, კმარა! მხოლოდ სიკვდილი
    მინდა,
არც პოეზია მატკბობს, არც მეგობრობა წმინ-
    და.
ეს რამდენიმე დღეა და რამდენიმე ღამე
არე-მიდამოს შხამავს ღრმა მწუხარების შხა-
    მი.
ჩამოიბუროს ზეცა, მისიც აღარა მჯერა —
მერის თვალებით იგი ვერ გაბრწყინდება, ვე-
    რა!

1914

WITH MARY'S EYES[3]

For several days and several nights
My heart has darkened been, closed tight.
As if a solitary cell,
A door that's locked with sealing wax.
No joy can reach my soul, no light
From skies that ever were so bright.
Each second of my being, my life
Has now become a desert wild.
For several days and several nights.
But now, you all, stop! Stand aside!
I long, long only for a Death,
Enjoying no Poesy, no friends.
The sphere is deeply poisoned here,
I ceased to trust the Heavens dear.
Let skies go dim! No more they'll shine
And brighten up with Mary's eyes!

წუხელი, დამით...

წუხელი, დამით ქარი დაჭქროდა
და დიდხანს, დიდხანს არ დამექინა;
მე მქონდა ბინა, თავშესაფარი,
მაგრამ ქარიშხალს არ ჰქონდა ბინა.

ხან კარებს უკან ატირდებოდა,
ხან დარაჯობდა სარკმელის წინა.
გადამიშალა თვალწინ წარსული
და მწარედ, მწარედ ამაქვითინა.

მისებრ პოეტი ვიყავ უცნობი —
ვეხეტებოდი სევდიან დამეს,
რამდენ ტკბილ ფიქრებს მოელო ბოლო,
რამდენ ოცნებას, რამდენ სიამეს!

წუხელი, დამით ქარი დაჭქროდა
და როცა დილით გამომეღვიძა,
ყვითელ ფოთლებს და დამსხვრეულ რტოებს
მიმოეფარათ ყამირი მიწა.

ბაღში გავეది... იქაც ბილიკზე
ფენილი იყო ფოთოლი რბილი,
და დიდხანს, დიდხანს ვხეტიალობდი
წარსულ სიზმარში გადაფრენილი.

1914

LAST NIGHT

Last night the wind, the wind whirled hard,
Long, long I could not fall asleep,
I had a home, a roof, a hut,
But never had a home the wind.

Sometimes the wind wept at the door,
Sometimes came closer to the panes,
It made me weep, it made me sob,
As told my past all full of pains.

And like the wind a poet I was,
And like the wind no one knew me,
Had gone by then the sweetest thoughts,
Had gone by then my dearest dreams.

Last night the wind, the wind whirled hard,
And when I woke up in the morn,
Leaves yellow and many a branch
Along the barren ground were thrown.

Went to the garden... on the path
I found again soft, yellow leaves,
I wandered lonely in the past,
That really was the last night dream.

როგორც სიზმარი

მე მივდიოდი, მე მივდიოდი
ყვავილთა შორის – ვით ნიავქარი,
მე სიყვარული მესიზმრებოდა
და მე ვიყავი – როგორც სიზმარი.

მე მივდიოდი, მე მოვდიოდი,
ზვირთივით სწრაფი, ზვირთივით ჩქარი.
ჩემი ოცნება სწვავდა ყვავილებს
და მე ვიყავი დილის ცისკარი.

მაგრამ ოცნებამ დამასნეულა,
სიმწრით აივსო ყვავილთ ნექტარი
და ძირს დაეშვა ფრთამომსხვრეული
ფიქრი ნაზი და დაუდევარი.

ყვავილთა შორის სიამის ნაცვლად
განადგურების ქანაობს ქარი,
და მწარე კვნესად მომესმის მხოლოდ
სალამოს ზარი... სალამოს ზარი.

შემოდგომაა... ბაღის ბილიკებს
მიმოფენია ფოთოლი მჭკნარი...
და მე მივდივარ, და მე მოვდივარ,
და მე ვარ ისე, როგორც სიზმარი.

1914

AS IF A DREAM

I walked, I walked among the flowers
As if I were air's wafting stream,
Oh, I dreamed of love at night hours,
And felt as if I were a dream.

I walked, I walked along the bowers
Like billows swift, like billows fast,
My hopes and dreams all burned the flowers,
I felt I was the morning star.

The realm of fancies made me ill,
No more my thoughts could reach the clouds,
Nectar of flowers – with poison filled,
Wingbroken thoughts flew slowly down.

Among the flowers no pleasure found,
The swinging wind of loss may tell,
As if the moans for me now sound
The chimes of evening, evening bells.

Now it is autumn, garden paths
Are covered all by withered leaves,
I walk, I walk along these paths,
I feel as if I were a dream.

ფოთლები

ჭკნება, ყვითლდება საბრალო ბალი,
ქარი უბერავს, ფოთლები ცვივა,
გამოურკვეველ მწუხარებაში
მზეს სული უწუხს და გული სტკივა.
ნოემბრის ქარმა ყვითელ ფოთლებით
კვალ-ბილიკებით გადაიარა,
ფოთლები სწყდება იმ გატაცებას
და შემოდგომის მეფობს იარა.

1914

LEAVES

The poor garden is sere and yellow,
The wind blows wild, no leaves are left,
But withered, and in vague sorrow
The sun's heart aches and gasps for breath.
November winds with yellow leaves
Have swept in furrows on their way,
The leaves break off from passion keen,
An open sore in autumn reigns.

რა სევდიან ნანას ამბობს ქარი...

რა სევდიან ზღაპარს ამბობს ქარი,
ამეშალა ჩვეულ ფიქრთა ჯარი.

დაიძინეთ, სურვილებო — კმარა!
კმარა ცრემლი, რაც რომ დაიღვარა.

დაიძინე შენც, იმედო, ჩემო,
ჩემო რწმენავ, ზეცავ და ედემო!

1915

HOW SAD THE LULLABY OF WINDS...

How sad are stories told by winds,
My thoughts are flowing still in streams,

No more desires, let all them sleep!
Enough are tears, oh, let them leave.

My faith and hope, do go to sleep,
Sleep Eden, skies and dearest dreams!

ვერხვები

ყოველთვის, როცა დააბერავს ქარი
და ნისლს მთებისას გაიფენს აფრად,
ვერხვის ფოთოლთა თეთრი ლაშქარი
აშრიალდება უშორეს ზღაპრად.

ზღაპარი იგი მათრობს და მხიბლავს
ჭველი ღვინის სმით, უღონოდ, მძაფრად,
სადღაც დაკარგულ ვარდს და გვირილებს
მოგონებებში ვიჭერ თანაბრად.

ეს იყო წინათ, დიდი ხნის წინათ...
სად, როდის, რისთვის? არ ვიცი, არა!
იყვნენ ოდესღაც და მიეძინათ...
ღელავს ფოთლების მწყობრი კამარა.

მას შემდეგ ბედი და იალქანი
ქარის სიმძიმით გადაიხარა,
შენ კი სადა ხარ ამდენი ხანი?
რისთვის, ან ვისთან? არ ვიცი, არა!

ეს იყო წინათ, დიდი ხნის წინათ,
ეს იყო ვერხვის ფოთლების კვნესა,
დრომ ყვავილებით დაგვაგვირგვინა,
მე პაჟი ვიყავ, ის კი — პრინცესა.

1915

ASPEN TREES[4]

When from the mounts the cold wind blows,
When mist is spreading like a sail,
An army of white aspen leaves
May rustle as a fairy tale.

This ancient tale makes thrilled and drunk,
And I am drunk with oldest wines,
In recollections then I grasp
The roses, daisies that were mine.

It was a long, long time ago,
Where, when, and why? I know not now!
They lived, but then, oh, passed away,
The leaping leaves sweep up and down.

Since then the fortune and the sail
Have bent beneath the heavy winds,
I long for you, I miss your face,
I never guess what all this means.

It was the moan of aspen trees,
Time fled so fast and much has changed,
Time crowned us two with flowery wreaths,
She was a princess, I – a page.

სადამო

მთის გაგიჟებულ რუებს,
ღვიით, ქენქით და ქვიშით,
გრიგალი დააყრუებს
მაცხოვრისადმი შიშით.

და დედოფალი ალვა,
ელვამ დალუნა ციემა;
ასე გავიდა გვალვა,
ასე მოვიდა წვიმა...

ჯვარი, ლომი და კურო
ფარშავანგების არის.
თვალთა ანგელოზთო შურო,
შენ, ღვთისმშობელო კარის!

ზარით ატეხილ გრიგალს
დავით ნარინის ჯვარი,
მარმარილოთა ფიქალს
გადააფარებს მძლავრი.

ან გაოცებას, რასაც
მარად ანათებს ძელი,
ისევ დაადებს რაზას
შემოღამების ცელი.

ან, როგორც ასომთავრულს,
მუდამ შევამჩნევ ცაზე,
სხვისთვის უხილავ-ფარულს
მე რად გელოდი ასე...

EVENING[5]

The mountain torrents madly rush,
With savin, sand, weeds wild,
By mighty gales they deafened are
With fright and awe of Christ.

The poplar that is a real queen,
By lightning is bent down,
The drought has gone, has gone away
To let the rains fall down.

Oh, the cross, the lion and the bull –
They are the peacocks' mates,
The eyes of angels envy you,
The Virgin of the Gate![6]

The dread and horror of the skies,
The sudden roar of thunders
By Narin's[7] cross of strength and might
Through marble slates'll be covered.

Or marvels of astonishment
Through faith in constant light,
Are latched as in no merriment
By scythes of the night.

Or as if the sacred letters,[8]
I ever see in skies,
All that is concealed from others,
I longed for you long while...

ჯვარზე გაკრული ელვა –
ეს ჩემი დაა ღურჯი,
ღურჯ ყვავილების თელვა –
ახალგაზრდობა ურჩი.

ჯვართან მისული სურო –
მარტოობაა ქნარის...
თვალთა ანგელოზთ შურო,
შენ, ღვთისმშობელო კარის!

1915

The lightning nailed across the cross –
Is sister blue of mine,
And trampling of those flowers blue
When young – a way of life.

When ivy climbs close to the cross,
It shows a lone harp's fate...
The eyes of angels envy you,
The Virgin of the Gate!

ბავშვობის დღეები

გაფრინდა ბავშვობის დღეები,
მინდვრები, ჭალები, ტყეები.
უეცრად მოვიდა შავებით
სხვა ბავში შორეულ დაბიდან.
მწუხარე ფერხულში ჩავებით
და თვალი ცრემლებმა დაბინდა.
ბალახი, მდინარე, ხეები,
დღეები, ბავშვობის დღეები.

1915

THE DAYS OF CHILDHOOD

The days of childhood are all fled,
With them the rivers and green belts,
All of a sudden there came a child,
All clad in black from distant climes.
We both joined a round dance of grief,
Our eyes with tears grew wet and dim.
The grass, the river, and the trees,
The days of childhood that we miss.

* * *

ელვარე და ლომფერი
იყო ცხრა ოქტომბერი,

მაგრამ თვალმა დათვალა
მზე ბევრი და ცხრათვალა...

ოჰ, მზით გადანაცხარო,
ცხრამუხა და ცხრაწყარო!..

რუსთაველი — ხანია,
ისიც ცხრა ანბანია...

გნება იყო ღვარული
ჩემი ცხრა სიყვარული.

ოდეს გნახე, ლომფერი
იყო ცხრა ოქტომბერი.

1915

* * *

Dazzling, coloured lion-like
Was October, on the ninth.

Eyes could count well in a while
Many a sun with nine eyes...

You, nine oaks, nine welling springs,
Are all touched by summer's heat!

Rustaveli[9] – course of time,
Spelled as well with letters nine...

And the passion, flown in floods,
Truly were those nine my loves.

When I met you, was the ninth,
Of that October lion-like.

შერიგება

ტოტებს ქარისას გადაჰყვა მარტი,
თეთრ განსაცმელში მე მოვირთვები
და წავალ ქარში, როგორც მოცარტი,
გულში სიმღერის მსუბუქ ზვირთებით.

დღეს ყველგან მზეა. ეხლა ამ ბაღებს
და მცინვარს, მაღალ ზრახვათა მეფეს,
მაისი ალით აახმახებს,
ვით შეყვარებულს და მეოცნებეს.

ჩვენ გვირგვინები გვაქვს ოდნავ მსგავსი,
ლამაზი შუქთა მარადი ნთებით:
მე — მსუბუქ დაფნის ფოთლებით სავსე,
მცინვარს — უმძიმეს იაგუნდებით.

ამაღლდი, სულო, თეთრ აკლდამაზე
მშვენიერების ლექსით მქებელი:
დღეს ყველგან მზეა და სილამაზე
სიკვდილთან ჩემი შემრიგებელი!

1915

RECONCILIATION

To windy branches when March yields
In white costume I will be clad,
Like Mozart, walking in the wind,
With waves of songs in heart I'll tread.

The sunny day is full of light
And icy Kaff,[10] the king of dreams,
Draws hues of iris from May skies,
As that to lover passion brings.

We both have crowns that are alike,
Eternal light shines over them:
My wreath of laurel is so light,
But Kaff's – of glacial heavy gems.

Oh, spirit, rise over tomb white
With praise of beauty in bard's words:
The sunny day is full of light
To reconcile me with my Death!

მთაწმინდის მთვარე

ჯერ არასდროს არ შობილა მთვარე ასე
    წყნარი!
მდუმარებით შემოსილი შემდამების ქნარი
ქროლვით იწევს ცისფერ ლანდებს და
    ხეებში აქსოვს...
ასე ჩუმი, ასე ნაზი ჯერ ცა მე არ მახსოვს!
მთვარე თითქოს ზამბახია შუქთა მკრთალი
    მძივით,
და მის შუქში გახვეული მსუბუქ სიზმარივით
მოსჩანს მტკვარი და მეტეხი თეთრად
    მოელვარე...
ოჰ! არასდროს არ შობილა ასე ნაზი მთვარე!
აქ ჩემს ახლო მოხუცის ლანდს სძინავს
    მეფურ ძილით,
აქ მწუხარე სასაფლაოს, ვარდით და
    გვირილით,
ეფინება ვარსკვლავების კრთომა მხიარული...
ბარათაშვილს აქ უყვარდა ობლად სიარული...
და მეც მოვკვდე სიმღერებში ტბის სევდიან
    გედად,
ოღონდ ვთქვა, თუ ლამემ სულში როგორ
    ჩაიხედა,
თუ სიზმარმა ვით შეისხა ციდან ცამდე
    ფრთები,
და გაშალა ოცნებათა ლურჯი იალქნები;
თუ სიკვდილის სიახლოვე როგორ
    ასხვაფერებს
მომაკვდავი გედის ჭანგთა ვარდებს და
    ჩანჩქერებს,

80

THE MOON OF MTATSMINDA[11]

Skies have never seen the moon tranquil, as is this!
A magic lyre seems serene in the dusk of bliss,
Calling forth on flight blue ghosts, binding them with
    trees...
I have never seen the skies tender, as are these!
The moon's like an iris bloom with pale beads of
    beams,
Gleaming gently all around as in night's light dreams
    –
The riverside[12] and the church[13] sparkle in white
    streams...
Skies have never seen the moon tender, as is this!
An old man's ghost,[14] so close to me, is in royal sleep,
And the cemetery's filled with a sorrow deep,
With a daisy[15] and a rose under merry stars...
Oh, these sites are haunted oft by the lonely bard...[16]
Fain would die I as a swan singing on the lake,
But to say how night has looked into soul in pains,
How the dream has spread its wings, reaching distant
    skies
When the sails of navy blue set are for the heights;
The waterfalls and roses change with swans' dying
    songs,
Tunes are altered when they feel that the end is close.

თუ როგორ ვგრძნობ, რომ სულისთვის, ამ
    ზღვამ რომ აღზარდა,
სიკვდილის გზა არრა არის, ვარდისფერ
    გზის გარდა;
რომ ამ გზაზე ზღაპარია მგოსანთ სითამამე,
რომ არასდროს არ ყოფილა ასე ჩუმი დამე,
რომ, ახრდილნო, მე თქვენს ახლო სიკვდილს
    ვეგებები,
რომ მეფე ვარ და მგოსანი და სიმღერით
    ვკვდები,
რომ წაჰყვება საუკუნეს თქვენთან ჩემი
    ქნარი...
ჯერ არასდროს არ შობილა მთვარე ასე
    წყნარი!

                                                    1915

For a soul so strong and bold, that in oceans rose,
Oh, the path of death is none but of sweet pink rose;
On this path, oh, as fairy tales are the poet's deeds,
There is none of darkened nights silent as is this,
And I say: I'll greet my death, being so close to
    ghosts,
With my songs I am dying – a king and a poet most,
Through the ages, but with you, harp of mine will
    live…
Skies have never seen the moon tranquil, as is this!

მერი

შენ ჯვარს იწერდი იმ ღამეს, მერი!
მერი, იმ ღამეს მაგ თვალთა კუდომა,
სანღომიან ცის ელვა და ფერი
მწუხარე იყო, ვით შემოდგომა!

აფეთქებული და მოცახცახე
იწოდა ნათელ ალთა კრებული,
მაგრამ სანთლებზე უფრო ეგ სახე
იყო იდუმალ გაფითრებული.

იწოდა ტაძრის გუმბათი, კალთა,
ვარდთა დიოდა ნელი სურნელი,
მაგრამ ლოდინით დაღალულ ქალთა
სხვა არის ლოცვა განუკურნელი.

მესმოდა შენი უგონო ფიცი...
მერი, ძვირფასო! დღესაც არ მჯერა...
ვიცი წამება, მაგრამ არ ვიცი:
ეს გლოვა იყო თუ ჯვარისწერა?

ლოდებთან ვიდაც მწარედ გოდებდა
და ბეჭდების თვლებს ქარში კარგავდა...
იყო ობლობა და შეცოდება,
დღესასწაულს კი ის დღე არ ჰგავდა.

ტაძრიდან გასულს ნაბიჯი ჩქარი
სად მატარებდა? ხედვა მიმქიმდა!
ქუჩაში მძაფრი დაჰქროდა ქარი
და განუწყვეტლად წვიმდა და წვიმდა.

84

MARY

You were married that night, Mary!
Mary, that night your eyes died all,
Hues and glints of skies so fairy
For autumn's sadness truly called!

Blasting and trembling, waving high,
Blazed brightness of the burning flames,
And paler than candles, all in light,
Seemed mystic colour of thy face.

Dome of the church and walls on fire,
Slow fragrance of roses was spread,
Prayer of women, of waiting tired,
Sounded but desperate and mad.

Faintly I heard your thoughtless vow...
Though never believed it... my dear!
Torture it was, but knew not how
Wedding turned into grief and tears.

And someone wailed close to the walls
Losing the gemstones in the wind...
Pity and loneliness there tolled,
It was not merriment indeed.

I left the church and quickly paced
Towards the roads! Could hardly see!
The heavy wind blew in my face,
It rained and rained, and waters streamed.

ნაბადი ტანზე შემოვიხვიე,
თავი მივანდე ფიქრს შეუწყვეტელს;
ოჰ! შენი სახლი! მე სახლთან იქვე
ღონე-მიხდილი მივაწექ კედელს.

ასე მწუხარე ვიდექი დიდხანს
და ჩემს წინ შავი, სწორი ვერხვეები
აშრიალებდნენ ფოთლებს ბნელხმიანს,
როგორც გაფრენილ არწივის ფრთები.

და შრიალებდა ტოტი ვერხვისა,
რაზე – ვინ იცის! ვინ იცის, მერი!
ბედი, რომელიც მე არ მეღირსა –
ქარს მიჰყვებოდა, როგორც ნამქერი.

სთქვი: უეცარი გასხივოსნება
რად ჩაქრა ასე? ვის ვევედრები?
რად აშრიალდა ჩემი ოცნება,
როგორც გაფრენილ არწივის ფრთები?

ან ცას ღიმილით რად გავცქეროდი,
ან რად ვიჯერდი შუქს მოკამკამეს?
ან „მესაფლავეს" რისთვის ვმღეროდი,
ან ვინ ისმენდა ჩემს „მე და ღამეს"?

ქარი და წვიმის წვეთები ხშირი
წყდებოდნენ, როგორც მწყდებოდა გული
და მე ავტირდი – ვით მეფე ლირი,
ლირი, ყველასგან მიტოვებული.

1915

I wrapped around my thick flint cape
And yielded to unceasing thoughts;
Your house! The place – to which I came,
Exhausted, leaned against the wall.

I stood in grief and did not quit,
In front of me stood aspen trees,[17]
Black, rustling with dark-sounding leaves
As if a soaring eagle's wings.

The aspen branches waved their leaves,
For what strove they? What did they mean?
The only message I could feel –
My luck was gone, gone with the wind.

Mary, pray tell me, sudden lustre,
Why died away? Whom shall I plead?
Why did my dream with noise rustle,
As if a soaring eagle's wings?

Why did I gaze at skies with smiles?
Why did I catch those beaming rays?
In vain sang my "Grave Digger's"[18] lines,
"The Night and I"[19] of doleful days?

The wind, the rain with drops so clear
Were breaking like the heart, all seared,
Anguish and pain no one could hear,
I wept, forlorn, as if King Lear.

ბზაში

I

ლურჯი აჩრდილი ცხელ ჰაერში დგას,
ისმის ნაცნობი ჭრჭოლა სიმინდის,
ზუზუნი გააქვს უბინაო სკას,
ოჰ! სამუდამოდ დაწყევლილ სინდისს.

სულს ენატრება ძველი ზღაპარი!
წარსული წმინდა იყო ამ ქალის —
როგორც სოფელში სამრეკლოს ზარი,
როგორც ყანებში ელვა ნამგალის.

როდის მოვიდა ცოდვების გროვა
და ჯოჯოხეთი... მითხარი, როდის?
დაბრუნდა სული და ვეღარ ჰპოვა
რამე, გარდა გზის და ცივი ლოდის.

II

მინდვრები, მთები და ზღვა ყანები
მზეზე ელვარებს ნამებით სველი,
კვლავ უზრუნველად მივექანები
უწვევად კარგი და ფეხმიშვები.

მოკლული ვიყავ უცხო ზმანებით,
დამწვარი ვიყავ ქალაქის ქაფით,
ხელები არ თრთის ხელთათმანებით!
სული არ ტირის შავი ნიღაბით!

88

ON THE ROAD

I

The blue ghost stands in the hot air,
From fields of maize the shiver's heard,
A homeless hive is humming there,
Oh, consciousness is forever cursed.

My soul is missing fairy tales!
The lady's past was pure and good –
Like chapel's bell on country vales,
Like lightning of a reaping hook.

When did the mass of sins arrive?
When did the Hell bring all its moans?
When soul came back, all it could find
Was lonely road and cold grave stone.

II

Vast cornfields, vales and mountains huge
Are shining bright with wet fresh dews,
I rush still careless and amused,
Unusually good and barefoot.

Oh, I was killed by strange, odd dreams,
And burned was I by city foam,
From gloves won't tremble hands indeed!
With black mask never weeps my soul!

III

მწვანე ჯალებში აფრინდა მწყერი,
გაფრინდა დალდა, მიჰქრის ტოროლა.
მწვანე ტალღების მიდის მეწყერი
ისმის ჯეჯილის მარათ-ქროლა.

სადმე ყრუ ადგილს დავესახლები
სხვა საუკუნის მგზავრი გვიანი,
სადაც იქნება ცოფი ნაკლები
და უფრო ნაკლებ ადამიანი.

ცა ლაჟვარდია... დღე არის თბილი,
მზე არის მწარე... გზა არის ცხელი.
კმარა! მოვშორდი შფოთიან ტფილისს!
არც მსურს მახსოვდეს მისი სახელი!

IV

და ერთადერთი ნაზი დარაჯი
გადიფრენს თვალწინ აჩრდილი მერის!
არამქვეყნიურ უზუნდარაში
გაიყოლიებს სულის სიბერეს.

არ დაბრუნდება ამ მხარეს ცეცხლი
წარსულთა დღეთა სხვანაირ მხარის;
ეხლა უმიზნოდ მიდის სიცოცხლე
და დაბრუნება მაინც მიხარის.

90

III

A quail has flown from deep green groves,
A snipe is up, high is a lark,
With these green waves a landslide moves,
Fan-flutter's heard of fresh grown grass.

I'll find a lonely place for home,
A traveller of other times,
Less rabies there to find, I hope,
To find fewer men to greet my sight.

The sky is azure... the day's warm,
The sun is bitter... road is hot,
From anxious city[20] I'm away!
I wish I never knew its name!

IV

But the only guardian of mine,
The shade, refined, of Mary flies!
To carry off through dance and smile
My worn-out soul to Heavens high.

The fire will never haunt the sites
To bring those memories aback;
The life, now aimless, flows and flies,
But I am happy to be back.

მხოლოდ ხანდახან ქარი შეარყევს
ოდნავ გადებულს კარებს ბაღისას,
შრიალი გააქეთ ძველებურ არყებს,
სხვა ცხოვრებისთვის თითქო მალვიძებს!

V

აქ მრავალია ცისფერი ფერი!
ეს ფერი მარად თვალს ეყვარება,
როგორც ქალწულის სახელი — მერი
არის ცისფერი და მწუხარება.

გახედე შორს მთებს! გახედე სერებს!
გახედე ტალღებს ჩაქსოვილს ტბაში.
ცისფერი ისე უცხოდ იფერებს
სამოსელს დღეთა ელვარებაში.

სული ექახის იმ უჩინარ ტყვეს,
ვისაც სიზმრებში უხსნიან ბაგეს,
იისთვის ეძებს იისფერ სიტყვებს
და ცისფერ სიტყვით ეძებს ციაგებს.

1916

From time to time the winds emerge
To shake an orchard gate at large,
The foliage shivers, rustle birches,
As if to wake me up for love.

V

Blue hues are many and they vary,
With them the eyes are ever in love,
As if the Virgin's name – Mary,
That's always blue, in sorrow plunged.

Look at the mountains and the hills!
Look at the lake with woven waves.
The blue attire now strangely fits
The brightness of the gaudy days.

Soul calls a captive who's unseen,
Whose lips they open on night dreams,
For violets violet words he seeks,
With light blue words he seeks the beams.

შენ ზღვის პირად

ზღვას სალამო ედებოდა მუქი.
შენ ზღვის პირად სჩანდი, როგორც შუქი.

მე პირველი მახსოვს შენი ნახვა,
გაოცება! მშვენიერი ზრახვა.

როგორც შორი ხომალდების ცქერა,
ვით პირველი გრძნობით გულის ძგერა.

ირხეოდა გამჭვირვალე რული
და მტკიოდა... და მტკიოდა გული.

იმ ხომალდებს სამუდამოდ გაჰყვა
გაოცება, მშვენიერი ზრახვა.

1916

WHEN YOU WALKED ALONG THE SEA

Darkness spread along the sea at night,
You appeared as a beam of light.

I remember first and foremost
A sudden stare! Beauty of my thoughts.

Like the sight of distant, distant ships,
And the beating of the heart that feels.

Somnolence was swinging with the mast,
Oh, how deeply... deeply ached my heart.

With those ships forever went offshore
A sudden stare, beauty of my thoughts.

შემოსილნი გამჯვირვალე ბლონდებით

შემოსილნო გამჯვირვალე ბლონდებით,
ყრმობის ქარნო, ნეტა რად მაგონდებით?

ტყდება გული, ერთხელ გაიბზარა რა,
არარა ბედს ჩემთვის არ აქვს არარა.

სასტიკია სული უამონდოთა,
განა ქვეყნად ბევრი რამე მინდოდა?

შემოსილნო გამჯვირვალე ბლონდებით,
ყრმობის ქარნო, ნეტა რად მაგონდებით?

1916

ALL DRESSED IN TRANSPARENT AND LACY VEILS

All dressed in transparent and lacy veils,
My days of youth, why haunt you me in gales?

My heart is breaking, it so often ached,
Ill-luck has nothing left for me to take.

The soul with weather foul is harsh and strict,
I never asked for much in life, indeed!

All dressed in transparent and lacy veils,
My days of youth, why haunt you me in gales?

თოვლი

მე ძლიერ მიყვარს იისფერ თოვლის
ქალწულებივით ხიდიდან ფენა,
მწუხარე გრძნობა ციგი სისოვლის
და სიყვარულის ასე მოთმენა.
ძვირფასო! სული მევსება თოვლით:
დღეები რბიან და მე გაბერდები!
ჩემს სამშობლოში მე მოვკვდე მხოლოდ
უდაბნო ლურჯად ნახავერდები.
ოჰ! ასეთია ჩემი ცხოვრება:
იანვარს მოძმედ არ ვეძნელები,
მაგრამ მე მუდამ მემახსოვრება
შენი თოვლივით მკრთალი ხელები.
ძვირფასო! ვხედავ... ვხედავ შენს ხელებს,
უღონოდ დახრილს თოვლთა დაფნაში.
იელვებს, ქრება და კვლავ იელვებს
შენი მანდილი ამ უდაბნოში...
ამიტომ მიყვარს იისფერ თოვლის
ჩვენი მდინარის ხიდიდან ფენა,
მწუხარე გრძნობა ქროლის, მიმოვლის
და ზამბახების წყებად დაწვენა.
თოვს! ასეთი დღის ხარებამ ლურჯი
და დაღალული სიზმრით დამთოვა.
როგორმე ზამთარს თუ გადავურჩი,
როგორმე ქარმა თუ მიმატოვა!
არის გზა, არის ნელი თამაში...
და შენ მიდიხარ მარტო, სულ მარტო!
მე თოვლი მიყვარს, როგორც შენს ხმაში
ერთ დროს ფარული დარდი მიყვარდა!
მიყვარდა მაშინ, მათრობდა მაშინ

SNOW

I'm fond of flakes of violet snow
Like virgins falling from a bridge,
A doleful touch of wetness cold
To bear the pains of Love in me.
My soul is, darling, filled with snow:
I'm getting old, my days run fast!
The land I paced in native home –
A desert blue with velvet paths.
This is my life: I'm not at odds
With friendly January at all,
But I shall ever have in thoughts
Your hands, your hands, as pale as snow.
Oh, darling! See I... see your hands
In laurel snowed, bent in relief,
I've seen your veil in desert lands,
Though disappearing in between...
That's why I love the violet snow,
Flakes falling from our river's bridge,
The layers of iris in low rows,
A doleful touch of winds that whirl.
It snows! And Lady Day in winter
Has covered me with tired blue dreams.
If I could but survive this winter,
If winds could spare me and leave!
There are the roads and games we meet...
You walk alone without recourse!
I love the snow as loved that grief,
Concealed in tender voice of yours!
Oh, then I loved, I truly loved

მუშიდი დღეების თეთრი ბროლება,
მინდვრის ფოთლები შენს დაშლილ თმაში
და თმების ქარით გამოქროლება.
მომწყურდი ეხლა, ისე მომწყურდი,
ვით უბინაოს — ყოფნა ბინაში...
თეთრი ტყეების მომყვება გუნდი
და კვლავ მარტო ვარ მე ჩემს წინაშე.
თოვს! ამნაირ დღის ხარებამ ლურჯი
და დადალული ფიფქით დამთოვა.
როგორმე ზამთარს თუ გადავურჩი!
როგორმე ქარმა თუ მიმატოვა!

1916

The peaceful days of crystal white,
In your loose hair the leaves were cast,
Your hair with winds was waving high.
I long for you, I long just like
A homeless – longs, longs for his home...
A flock of forests, that's all white,
Now haunts me and I'm still alone.
It snows! And Lady Day in winter
Has covered me with tired blue sheets.
If I could but survive this winter!
If winds could spare me and leave!

ცამეტი წლის ხარ

ცამეტი წლის ხარ და შენი ტყვეა
ჭადარა გულის ზმანება ავი, –
ჩააწყვეთ რიგში ცამეტი ტყვია,
ცამეტჯერ უნდა მოვიკლა თავი!

გაივლის კიდევ ცამეტი წელი,
მოახლოვდება გზა ოცდაექვსი,
მოცელავს მადალ ზამბახებს ცელი,
ატირდება დრო და ჩემი ლექსი.

ოჰ, როგორ მიდის ახალგაზრდობა –
დაუნდობელი სურვილი ლომის!
და ყოველივე როგორ ნახდება,
როცა ახლოა მზე შემოდგომის.

1916

YOU ARE THIRTEEN

You are thirteen and have enslaved
An evil dream in this grey heart, –
I'll kill myself thirteen times, hey!
Load thirteen bullets one by one.

Thirteen more years will fly with time,
The road of twenty-six will start,
Iris will fall beneath the scythe,
Time and my poems will in tears burst.

Time goes, time flies, with time flies youth,
The ruthless will of lions all goes!
Soon all seems tender, all is soothed,
When autumn sun is now so close.

დროშები ჩქარა!

გათენდა. ცეცხლის მზე აენთო, აცურდა...
დროშები ჩქარა!
თავისუფლება სულს ისე მოსწყურდა,
ვით დაჭრილ ირმების გუნდს – წყარო
    ანკარა...
დროშები ჩქარა!

დიდება ხალხისთვის წამებულ რაინდებს,
ვინც თავი გასწირა, ვინც სისხლი დაღვარა.
მათ ხსოვნას ქვეყანა სანთლებად აინთებს...
დროშები ჩქარა!

დიდება, ვინც კიდევ გვაპრძოლებს იმედით,
ვინც მედგრად დახვდება მტრის რისხვა-
    მუქარას...
გათენდა! შეერთდით, შეერთდით, შეერთდით!
დროშები, დროშები... დროშები ჩქარა!

                                    1917

KEEP BANNERS HIGH!

It has just dawned!
The fiery sun is soaring in the sky...
Keep banners high!
The soul's so thirsty for freedom and light,
As wounded deer are for welling springs wild...
Keep banners high!

Glory to martyrs who ventured in fights,
Who shed the blood and sacrificed their lives.
Whose memory for candles willl ever glare bright...
Keep banners high!

Glory to those who encourage no fright,
Encounter the enemy's ire of blight...
It has just dawned! You all, unite, unite!
Keep banners, the banners... Keep banners high!

* * *

მზეო თიბათვისა, მზეო თიბათვისა,
ლოცვად მუხლმოყრილი გრაალს შევედრები.
იგი, ვინც მიყვარდა დიდი სიყვარულით,
ფრთებით დაიფარე — ამას გევედრები.
ტანჯვა-განსაცდელში თვალნი მიურიდენ,
სული მოავლინე ისევ შენმიერი,
დილა გაუთენე ისევ ციურიდან,
სული უმანკოთა მიეც შვენიერი.
ხანმა უნდობარმა, გზა რომ შეელდება,
უხვად მოიტანა სისხლი და ცხედრები,
მძაფრი ქარტეხილი მას ნუ შეეხება,
მზეო თიბათვისა, ამას გევედრები.

1917

* * *

Sun of Ærraliða,[21] sun of Ærraliða,
Knelt down in prayer, I'm as Holy Grail.[22]
Spare the one whom I so dearly loved,
Shelter her with your wings, I plead and pray.
In torments and perils, you veil her eyes,
Send her again the spirit that glares,
Let the blue skies still bring her morns bright,
Endow her with soul that's guiltless and fair.
Times, that were hard and cruel, to paint the road
Brought plenty of blood and many killed,
Save her from harsh gales, those winds with moans,
Oh, sun of Ærraliða, this I entreat.

არ არის იგი იმდენად ტკბილი

არ არის იგი იმდენად ტკბილი
დრო, დაფარული ცეცხლის ენებით,
მაგრამ არც ისე მწარე აქვს კბილი
საწამლავებით და შეჩვენებით.
მან შეაჩვია სოფელს სატანა,
ჯოჯოხეთური ალი ქურების,
რათა შემდეგში შესძლოს აგანა
უფრო საშინელ განადგურების.

1917

IT'S NE'ER AS SWEET AS IT MAY SEEM

It's ne'er as sweet as it may seem,
When Time's covered with flames of fire,
But not so bitter are its teeth
With poison, cursing, ill desire.
Time brought the devil from his Hell
To make accustomed to the world,
The fires of forges to withstand,
Destruction coming out of hand.

* * *

იმ ვარდისფერ ატმებს მოვიგონებ კვლავ...
იმგვარადვე მდევ... იმგვარადვე მკლავ.

ო, როგორ მომწყურდი! მწუხარეა ღდე.
იმგვარივე ცა, იმგვარივე ხე...

იგივ ქარი დაჰქრის, იღუნება ბზა.
იმგვარივე მზე, იმგვარივე გზა.

ძლიერ... ძლიერ... ძლიერ... ვეტყვი ზენა ქარს
იმგვარივე ხმით იმგვარივე ზარს.

1917

* * *

Peach-blossom clings still to my mind.
You haunt again and kill me, why?

I long for you! And mourns the day.
The sky, the way – they seem the same.

The willow bows, the same wind blows.
The same sun shines, same is the road.

Be strong... strong... strong... I say to winds
With voice the same and similar ring.

* * *

(ძღვნად ოლ-ოლს)

ორი ზღვა შეხვდა ერთიმეორეს,
ერთი — ქარიშხლის, მეორე — მშვიდის,
მათ აღტაცებით განიმეორეს,
რომ დრო ახალი იმედით მიდის.
ფეერიულ ნავს სცილდება კორდი,
ამაყი ლორდი დგას, დროა ძველი.
ბაირონს უსმენს მერი ჩავორტი
და ფერადებში მისცურავს შელლი.
ტალღები სთვლემენ, ვით შორი ბედი
და ნაპირებთან მისული ნავი,
ზვირთებთან ერთად ოხრავს მილედი
და პოეზიის დაიძრა ზვავი.

1917

* * *

(to Ol-ol)[23]

The two great seas have met each other.[24]
Stormy is one, calm is the other.
Both in excitement are saying anew,
That time is going now with hopes all new.
Green turf's parting from a fairy boat,
The proud lord is standing, time is old.
To Byron's words is harking Mary.[25]
Through colours fine is floating Shelley.
A boat is swinging low by the shore,
The waves're dozing like a fate remote.
With billows high is sighing my lady,
A snow slide of Poesy is gliding.

ანგელოზს ეჭირა ბრძელი პერგამენტი

ანგელოზს ეჭირა გრძელი პერგამენტი,
მწუხარე თვალებით მიწას დაჰყურებდა.
მშვიდობით, მშვიდობით! ამაოდ დაგენდე,
ელვარე სალამოვ აღმას საყურეთა!
ბაგეთა ლოცვაო, დიდება და ძეგლო,
უთუოდ მახსენებ ოდესმე... ოდესმე!
გრაალის კოშკები, ლიდიის სამრეკლო
შენს ფეხთქვეშ დაიმსხვრა და გლოვა
    მომესმა.
ოჰ! როგორ გაფითრდა ციურთა თანადი
ოცნება, ნახაზი საგანთა უარით,
ღრუბელი ფერადი და ალვა ტანადი,
რომელსაც აზიის ცით გადაუარეთ.
ანგელოზს ეჭირა გრძელი პერგამენტი
და ფოთლებს ისროდა სიფითრე ბარათის.
ამაოდ დაგენდე, და ჩვენ ერთმანეთი
ამაოდ გვინდოდა! მშვიდობით მარადის!
ქარვათა მორევში დაეშვა ფარდები –
სალამო კანკალებს შიშით და რიდობით,
სალამო ნელდება და კვდება ვარდები...
მშვიდობით, მშვიდობით, მშვიდობით!..

1917

AN ANGEL WAS HOLDING A LONG PARCHMENT

An angel was holding a long parchment,
With sorrowful eyes gazed down on the earth,
Farewell, farewell! I trusted you in vain,
The evening's sparkling with earrings of gems!
Prayer of lips, the fame and the monument,
Will certainly mention me one day well!
The towers of Grail[26] and the Lydian[27] chapel,
That are all destroyed at your feet as well.
Oh, I heard the sounds of grieving and plight,
Paler grew suddenly the heaven-sent dream,
All striped along with refusals of life,
Tall poplars and fair clouds with cheerful beams
Which we then flew over through Asian skies,
Paleness of the letter cast on the leaves.
The angel still gazed with sorrowful eyes,
We longed for each other in vain indeed.
The curtain fell down in gulfs of amber,
Evening is trembling in fright, disarray,
Roses are dying and twilight is tendered…
Farewell, farewell, farewell to thee, away!..

სილაჟვარდე ანუ ვარდი სილაში

დედაო ღვთისავ, მზეო მარიამ!
როგორც ნაწვიმარ სილაში ვარდი,
ჩემი ცხოვრების გზა სიზმარია
და შორეული ცის სილაჟვარდე.

შემოიღამებს მთის ნაპრალები,
და თუ როგორმე ისევ გათენდა –
ღამენათევი და ნამთვრალევი,
დაღლილ ქალივით მივალ ხატებთან!

ღამენათევი და ნამთვრალევი
მე მივეყრდნობი სალოცავ კარებს,
შემოიჭრება სიონში სხივი
და თეთრ ოლარებს ააელვარებს.

და მაშინ ვიტყვი: აჰა! მოვედი
გედი დაჭრილი ოცნების ბაღით!
შეხედე! დასტკბი ყმაწვილურ ბედის
დაღლილ ხელებით, წამებულ სახით!

შეხედე! დასტკბი! ჩემი თვალები,
წინათ რომ ფეთქდნენ ცვრებით, იებით, –
ღამენათევი და ნამთვრალევი
სავსეა ცრემლთა შურისძიებით!

დასტკბი! ასეა ყველა მგოსნები?
შენს მოლოდინში ასეა ყველა?
სული, ვედრებით განაოცები,
შენს ფერხთ ქვეშ კვდება, როგორც პეპელა.

AZURE-LAND AS ROSE IN SAND[28]

Ave Maria, Sunny Virgin!
As if a rose in rain-soaked sand,
My life's dream, in sleep imagined,
Of skies remote and azure-land.

The night descends on mountain sides,
And if the sun can ever rise –
Then as a weary woman sighing,
I'll walk to icons greeting light!

And after sleepless drunken nights
I'll rest myself on sacred doors,
Sunbeams will enter, burning bright,
Illuminating snow-white stoles.

Then I will say: I've come, a swan,
Wounded by the garden of dreams!
Look and enjoy! The fate of one
With worn out hands, exhausted mien!

Look and enjoy! What has become
Of eyes that flashed with violets, dews, –
From sleepless drunken nights in sum,
Are filled with tears of vengeful hues!

All bards! Do they the same fate share,
As tortured thus by your retreat?
And then the soul in wonder-pray,
Like butterflies dies at your feet.

სად არის ჩემთვის სამაგიერო?
საბედნიერო სად არის სული?
ვით სამოთხიდან ალიგიერი,
მე ჯოჯოხეთით ვარ დაფარული!

და როცა ბედით დაწყევლილ გზაზე
სიკვდილის ლანდი მომეჩვენება,
განსასვენებელ ზიარებაზე
ჩემთან არ მოვა შენი ხსენება!

დავიკრეფ ხელებს და გრიგალივით
გამაქანებენ სწრაფი ცხენები!
დამენათები და ნამთვრალევი
ჩემს სამარეში ჩავესვენები.

დედაო ღვთისავ, მზეო მარიამ!
როგორც ნაწვიმარ სილაში ვარდი,
ჩემი ცხოვრების გზა სიზმარია
და შორეული ცის სილაჟვარდე!

1917

I guess, this fortune never meant
To make my soul instead all bright,
With Hell am I now overwhelmed
Like Dante was in Paradise!

When on my way, accursed by fate,
I see the ghost of cruel Death,
I'll never meet your name or face
With Eucharist at my last breath!

I'll cross my hands, like hurricane
Will horses forward me ahead!
From drunken sleepless nights I came,
Now rush to grave – my final bed.

Ave Maria, Sunny Virgin!
As if a rose in rain-soaked sand,
My life's dream, in sleep imagined,
Of skies remote and azure-land!

შინდისის ჯადრებს

ორო ჯადარო, წყვილო ჯადარო,
შემოხვეულნო შუქთა ბადრებით, –
ო, მე არ ვიცი, რას შეგადაროთ,
ან უცხოეთში რად მენატრებით?

კვლავ გახვევიათ ოქროს ზეწარი
და შემოდგომის მკრთალი ბლონდები?
მე, უთვისტომო და გარეწარი,
თქვენ გაგიხსენებთ და დავლონდები.

თქვენთან რბიოდნენ ნათელნი დღენი,
ლოცვა ბავშვური, ფერი გედური,
ეხლა რად მესმის შრიალი თქვენი,
როგორც ტირილი და საყვედური?

1917

TO THE PLANE TREES OF SHINDISI[29]

For you, a pair of tall plane-trees,
I'll never find a true compare,
Embraced you were with full light beams,
I long for you in distant wheres.

Are you still wrapped in golden sheets
And autumn brings a thin pale lace?
A profligate without a kin,
I'll think of you in gloomy ways.

Nice days with you were running fast,
Those childish prayers and hues of swans,
But why in ears your rustle lasts
As if lament and a reproach?

სილაში ვარდი

ხედავ ამ ყვავილს? გაზაფხულის მზე
რადაც უცნაურ გრძნებას ახვევდა...
მან არ იცოდა ყოფნა მშფოთარე,
მან არ იცოდა მწუხრი და სევდა.
ის ქარიშხალს არ მოუწყვეტია,
რადგან ხალისით უცქერდა ზეცა;
არა, ის მშობელ ბუჩქს თავისთავად
მოსწყდა და მტვრიან გზაზე დაეცა.
აღარ უღიმის ეხლა მზე ყვავილს
და არც ყვავილი ამშვენებს მდელოს;
ნება აქვს ზეცას, სულ დააჭკნოს ის,
ბრბოსაც ნება აქვს, ფეხით გასთელოს!

1917

A ROSE IN SAND[30]

Look at this flower! The sun in spring
Created magic over her...
She[31] never knew a troubled being,
Of sorrow never overheard.
She was not plucked by storm or wind,
She viewed the skies with joy the most,
It happened so that from a twig
It fell down on a dusty road.
No more the rose fresh lawns adorns,
No more the sun now smiles on her;
The skies have power to fade her all,
And mobs have power to trample her!

მას გახელილი დარჩა თვალები

მზეო თიბათვის, ყოფნა უმზეო!
მზე მიიცვალა ლია თვალებით!
ის მიიცვალა რადაც უმწეო
და საოცარი გარდაიცვალებით!

მას გახელილი დარჩა თვალები,
ოჰ! გახელილი დარჩა თვალები!
ის უცხო მხარეს გარდაიცვალა
და გახელილი დარჩა თვალები!

და ეს თვალები საღამოთა ხმას
უსმენდნენ ტანჯვით და მოკრძალებით:
მას გახელილი დარჩა თვალები,
ოჰ, გახელილი დარჩა თვალები!

რა ხდება იქით! საიდან ისმის
მგლოვიარეთა ქნართა: "მშვიდობით"?
უეცრად სწყვეტენ სიმები სიცილს
უამინდობით... უამინდობით!

საიდან ისმის ჭყმი გალობა
და უღონობა სუნთქვის შემწყდარის,
წამების წყნარი წარმავალობა
და მოგონება ძვირფასი მკვდარის?

მიდის ზაფხული... ბაღში, მდელოში
სისინებს სიო, შრიალებს ნეშო,
მე ისევ აქ ვარ... საქართველოში!
რისთვის, ძვირფასო! რისთვის, ნუგეშო?

124

HER EYES STAYED OPEN AS SHE DIED

Sun of Ærraliða,[32] sunless life!
The sun has died with open eyes!
She[33] died with somewhat helpless death,
It was a strange and feeble death!

Her eyes stayed open! Oh, her eyes!
Her eyes stayed open as she died.
She died afar in foreign lands,
With eyes still open lay she dead!

Her eyes then harked to voice of Eves
With shyness, torture and goodwill:
Her eyes stayed open! Oh, her eyes,
Her eyes stayed open as she died!

But what is there! From where is heard
With mourning harps, "Farewell, Farewell"?
The weather's foul... Oh, what a day!
The strings ceased smiling on their way.

From where the silent chant is heard
And weakness of the broken breath,
And tranquil transience of the time,
Remembrance of the one who died?

The summer lapses from the fields,
The foliage rustles, breathes breeze,
I'm still in Georgia, still at home!
For what, my dear! For what, my hope?

და ეს თვალები სერაფიმთა ხმას
უსმენდნენ ტანჯვით და მოკრძალებით,
მას გახელილი დარჩა თვალები,
ოჰ! გახელილი დარჩა თვალები!

მივალ, მიმყვება მე შენი ცქერა
და ხავერდებზე ეცემა ჩრდილი,
ყველგან უჩინრად ტირის ცრერა,
თვალები ცი31 და გახელილი.

ღირდა თუ არა სხვა სიცოცხლეზე
ოცნება ჩუმი და ფერმიხდილი?
მე გზა არ ვიცი უახლოესი:
ერთადერთი გზა არის სიკვდილი.

მას გახელილი დარჩა თვალები,
ოჰ, გახელილი დარჩა თვალები!
ის უცხო მხარეს გარდაიცვალა
და გახელილი დარჩა თვალები!

1918

126

To seraphs' singing harked these eyes,
Where torture was with kindness twined,
Her eyes stayed open! Oh, her eyes,
Her eyes stayed open as she died!

I pace, but followed by your glance,
And shadows fall on velvet paths,
Oh, Ceres sobs wherever by stealth,
Her icy eyes stayed open still.

And was it worth to dream a while,
In silence though, of other life?
Of shortest ways in search am I:
The only way is way to die.

Her eyes stayed open! Oh, her eyes!
Her eyes stayed open as she died.
She died afar in foreign lands,
With eyes still open lay she dead!

სტიროდა სული ცისფერ ღვინოებს

სტიროდა სული ცისფერ ღვინოებს,
ღვინო ეძებდა სულ სხვას პირიქით
და შემდეგ უცნობ პიანინოებს
ატრიალებდა განჯგის ლირიკით.

როგორც მრავალი ვარდების მფენი,
მას სული ჰქონდა უხვად ციური,
მასში მრავალი იყო შოპენი
და პაგანინი ფანტასტიური.

მას საქართველომ გადაუზნიქა
ვერხვები შორი ალაზანისა
და აი, ეხლა მისი მუსიკა
ჩვენი ისლების რხევამ დანისლა.

მშვენიერია ეფექტი მისი
იქ, სადაც სიტყვა თავდება ძველი,
ოდეს თავისი და არა სხვისი
ცრემლებით თვალი უბრწყინავს სველი.

1919

THE SOUL WEPT OUT WITH LIGHT BLUE WINES

The soul wept out with light blue wines,
But wine then searched for someone else
And whirled the piano keys meanwhile
With lyric of tormenting tense.

As if all spreading fair roses
The soul was full of Heaven's spell,
Contained much of Chopin's music
And Paganini's fancy realm.

Tall aspen trees of Alazani[34]
Bent low in Georgia on his way,
And music then, all of a sudden,
Got misty through our Carex waves.

Effect is fine, overwhelming,
Where end those words, all worn and old,
The eyes in tears, gently melting,
Are sparkling wet but never cold.

პოეზია – უპირველეს ყოვლისა!

სული გვქონდეს უსპეტაკეს თოვლისა!
მეგობრებო, სიკვდილამდის მექნება
მხოლოდ ერთი სიხარულის შეგნება:
პოეზია – უპირველეს ყოვლისა!

თავდადებულ ბრძოლებისთვის ნახევარ
გზად დადლილი არვის არ ვუნახივარ,
მარად მანთებს შუქი სვეტიცხოვლისა:
პოეზია – უპირველეს ყოვლისა!

სიკვდილივით მარადია სურვილი
მთელი ქვეყნის სიმდერებით მოვლისა,
ყველაფერში შუქით შემობურვილი:
პოეზია – უპირველეს ყოვლისა!

თუ სამშობლო მაინც არ მომეფეროს,
მე მოვკვდები, როგორც პოეტს შეჰფერის.
სიმდერები ხალისის და ბრძოლისა:
პოეზია – უპირველეს ყოვლისა!

1920

POESY, POESY – FIRST AND FOREMOST!

To have a soul that's purer than the snow!
Dear friends, till death I promise to be true
To boundless joy that ever keeps and proves:
Poesy, Poesy – first and foremost!

No one has ever seen me on the way
Half tired was I in wars for dearest goals,
Inspired as ever by the beam of faith.[35]
Poesy, Poesy – first and foremost!

Like Death eternal is my dearest wish
To pace the world with sweetest, sweetest songs,
In every instance full of light that is:
Poesy, Poesy – first and foremost!

But if my country fails to treat me well,
Yes! I'll die a death, a poet's name deserves.
With songs of merriment, of fights ne'er lost:
Poesy, Poesy – first and foremost!

ცხოვრება ჩემი

ცხოვრება ჩემი უანკარეს ღვინის ფერია,
იგი ელვარებს, საბოლოოდ დაშრება ვიდრე,
მასში დიდება პოეტისა მე დავიმკვიდრე,
რომლის გარეშე — უკვდავებაც არაფერია.
თეთრი დღეების ისევ ისე მიჰყვება დასი,
არ მომწყინდება სადღეგრძელოდ ავწიო თასი
თქვენი, რომელთა გატაცება... მხოლოდ...
    ჟინია.
მე არც წარსულის, არც მომავლის არ
    მეშინია.

1922

MY LIFE

My life's like the purest, purest wine,
It shines and dazzles till it's all dried up,
A poet's fame through it established I,
Save this, immortality ne'er lasts.
I'm never tired to toast to you, for whom
A passion... is a mere whim... that tortures,
A whole host of days, white days, now moves,
Feared neither for my past nor future.

იყო

იყო ბურუსი გაურღვეველი
და კაკანებდა ტყვიისმფრქვეველი.

დღემ მოღუშულმა წარბი შეხარა,
დაცლილ ქუჩებზე მკვდრები ეყარა.

უცებ მადალი ცეცხლი ავარდა
და ბნელი ცისკენ გაინავარდა.

ცეცხლი ძლიერი დიდხანს ვინახე,
როს იმედები სხვა დავინახე.

ეს მინდა ვუთხრა მიეთ-მოეთებს:
მე ქარში ვიყავ, როცა პოეტებს

თქვენთვის საყვარელ ბულბულ-მდელოში,
ტკბილად გეძინათ საქართველოში.

1923

YOU WOULDN'T

You would not break through that thick fog,
A machine-gun all cackled hot.

A gloomy day in worry frowned,
The empty streets – with dead around.

Out of a sudden a fire upblazed,
Towards dark sky it freely chased.

I held that fire in heart for long,
As viewed the hopes for which I longed.

Let now the windbags hear me well:
When weathered I in winds like hell,

On meadows with nightingales sweet,
You, poets of Georgia, were asleep.

ქარი ჰქრის...

ქარი ჰქრის, ქარი ჰქრის, ქარი ჰქრის,
ფოთლები მიჰქრიან ქარდაქარ...
ხეთა რიგს, ხეთა ჯარს რკალად ხრის,
სადა ხარ, სადა ხარ, სადა ხარ?..
როგორ წვიმს, როგორ თოვს, როგორ თოვს,
ვერ გპოვებ ვერასდროს... ვერასდროს!
შენი მე სახება დამდევს თან
ყოველ დროს, ყოველთვის, ყოველგან!..
შორი ცა ნისლიან ფიქრებს სცრის...
ქარი ჰქრის, ქარი ჰქრის, ქარი ჰქრის!..

1924

WHIRLS THE WIND

Whirls the wind, whirls the wind, whirls the wind
And the leaves whirl from wind still to wind…
Rows of trees, lines of trees bend in arch,
Where art thou, where art thou, why so far?..
How it rains, how it snows, how it snows,
Where to find, where to find... Never know!
But pursued, but pursued by your eyes
All the time, everywhere, every time!..
Distant skies drizzle thoughts mixed with mist…
Whirls the wind, whirls the wind, whirls the wind!..

პროლოგი 100 ლექსის

რა საოცარი დასრულდა წლები!
მეფეთა წყება გაჰქრა, ვით ლანდი,
მოშორდნენ ტახტებს: ვილჰელმი, კარლოს,
ნიკოლოოზი და ფერდინანდი.
მაგრამ მწუხარედ მათზე კი არა,
სხვაზე იფიქრებს მარტიროლოგი:
იმ საშინელ წელს — პოეტი-მეფე —
გარდაიცვალა ალექსანდრ ბლოკი,
ჰანგების მეფე — დიდი სენ-სანსი
და დირიჟორი ნიკიშ მძლავრი...
ეკლიან გზაზე დაეცა ბევრი —
მხოლოდ მე ერთი გადავრჩი მგზავრი,
რომ გამომეცლო ჯერარსმენილი
ქარტეხილები ცეცხლთა ფენისა
და მომეტანა საქართველოში
სიმღერა ქვეყნის გადარჩენისა!

1925

PROLOGUE FOR 100 POEMS

What years of wonders by now have ended!
Vanished a host of kings as a shadow,
Wilhelm, and Karl, Nikoloz, Ferdinand,
Yes, all of them were delivered from thrones.
Not over them, but over the different
A martyrologist will mourn again:
That dreadful year, oh, you know what happened?
King of poets – Alexandr Blok passed away.
Died Saint-Saëns, a great man – the king of tunes,
And Nikisch, a powerful conductor died.
Many have fallen on the road of thorns...
Harsh were the years, the years severe and wild.
I'm the only traveller that survived,
To pass the fiery gales, yet never heard,
To bring to Georgia sacred song of might,
As a saviour, a saviour of the world.

ეჯახებიან პლანეტები ერთი მეორეს

რბიან დღეები. სული დაექქება უშორეს
    ხაზებს,
სივრცეებს მზეთა უშორესთა სპექტრო
    ანაზებს,
მე ვცხოვრობ გულით შფოთიანად მცემარეთ
    შორის,
რომელმაც დაგმო სიმშვიდეთა მკრთალი
    სახება...
იქ სიმძაფრეა და შეკახება:
ეჯახებიან პლანეტები ერთი მეორეს.

                                        1925

140

PLANETS CLASH

Days run. The soul is now in search of farthest lines,
Spaces of farthest suns are tendered by their lights,
I live among those troubled, whose hearts are beating
    hard,
Who have denied by calmness, so pale, to be loved...
All is so harsh and utmost, loud noise of calls's heard:
At war are now the planets, the planets now clash.

ავადმყოფს

შეხედე: ვარდნი მშვიდი თვალებით
სძლებენ ნარიდნი მსუბუქ ძალებით,
ვარდები უფრო კეთილშობილი
კვდებიან სწრაფი გარდაცვალებით.
გაყვითლებულა მიდამო-არე
შემოხარცული მთებით მოარე.
ფაენმა სიცილით მოვლო მთა-ველი
და არა ერთი მოჭკლა ყვავილი.
შემოდგომაა ტკივილი ჩუმი
და ხელის გულთა ნაზი ქავილი.
ყვითელო, ჩემო ყვითელო ვარდო,
შთაენილხარ მარტო, სრულიად მარტო.
რითმების გარდა არაფერი მაქვს...
რითი გაგართო? როგორ გაგართო?

1925

TO A SICK PERSON

Oh, look at the roses with their quiet eyes,
With gentle, modest strength they have survived.
But other roses of much nobler sort,
They die so fast, the sight of them is gone.
The ambience, that's yellow all around,
Is now surrounded by naked-bare mounts.
A faun in laughter paces slopes and fields
And on the way so many flowers kills.
It's autumn now and silent is the pain,
A tender itch I feel in palms so pale.
How shall I please, how to amuse you, how?
All withered, withered, left alone you're now.
My yellow rose, oh, yellow rose of mine,
I guess, you know, that all I have – are rhymes...

სასაფლაონი

სარკოფაგიდან დგება მუმია. რა სიჩუმეა.
ჰაერი ლურჯი აბრეშუმია.
ორხიდეები ეცემა ნილოსს,
როს მხურვალდება ქვიშაზე კვნესის,
უნდა, რომ სული არ მიისილოს,
უნდა სამარე ჰპოვოს რამზესის.
ის იყო მეფე. ეხლაა მტვერი,
რომ საუკუნეთ რიგი გარიყოს,
არ შეუძლია იყოს პირფერი,
არ შეუძლია მტვერი არ იყოს.
და საუკუნეთ რიგს თვლის მუმია:
მზიანი დღეა თუ სამუშია.

1925

GRAVEYARDS

A mummy rises. Oh, look there!
What silence. Blue silk is the air.
A sarcophagus. All is quiet.
Orchids are falling on the Nile,
The heat is groaning and strives
To free the soul from sand meanwhile,
To find the coffin – Ramses lay.
He was the king, but now is clay,
Hypocrisy is not his way,
He can't be other than mere clay.
A mummy counts the ages there:
A sunny day or simoom[36] flares.

მე არა ერთხელ მქონია ფრთები

მე არაერთხელ მქონია ფრთები
თავბრუდამხვევი სიმაღლით მქროლი,
ლურჯი ტრიალით ბრუნავდენ მთები
და ირყეოდა ლაჟვარდი ბროლი.

და არა ერთხელ მიგრძვნია მაშინ,
რომ ის მიწები სხვა მიწებია,
დამვიწყებია მოწამლვა შხამით,
მაგრამ კივილში გამღვიძებია.

ვყოფილვარ ბევრჯერ სიკვდილის პირად,
ომში მინახავს ცეცხლის ვარდები,
იმ სიმაღლეებს ვიგონებ ხშირად:
არ მავიწყდება ის ლაჟვარდები.

1925

I HAVE HAD WINGS NOT ONLY ONCE

I have had wings not only once
To dash me swift to giddy heights,
The mounts revolved in dark blue whirls,
The azure crystal swinging bright.

And I have felt not only once
Those lands are different and strange,
I have forgotten that poisoned was,
I used to shriek myself awake.

I used to face the Death, the end,
In wars the fiery roses met,
Those heights I often recollect:
Those azure skies I can't forget.

იარე, კაცი შენ აღარ გქვიან!

გასწიე! დამე ემშვება ზეწრად,
მწარედ შრიალებს ტყეთა კალთები,
მახლობელ დემონს იგრძნობ უეცრად
და შიშის ჩრდილით აკანკალდები.

იარე! გაჰყევ გზას შორით შორისს,
მაისთა ცეცხლი შენ არ გაოსებს,
მწუხარებათა ულევთა შორის
ისევე ხედავ ახალ ქაოსებს.

გააზელ თვალებს — იქნება გვიან,
დახუჭავ, მაინც ცა არ ენთება...
იარე, კაცი შენ აღარ გქვიან,
შენთვის არასდროს არ გათენდება.

რა უყავ შენს სულს, ოდესმე კეთილს,
ქვეყნად რომ სურდა ცეცხლის მოდება?
ეხლა იმავ სულს დაღლილს, დაფლეთილს,
დახედავ და არ შეგეცოდება.

იკივლებ მაშინ, მაგრამ არსიდან
არ გიპასუხებს უდაბურება,
იარე! გზები უშინაარსო
ისევ ბურუსით დაიბურება.

1925

WALK FORWARD! YOU, NO MORE A MAN!

Be off! The night in sheets descends,
Dark woods in bitter rustle fight,
The kindred demon will be felt
To make you tremble in a fright.

Walk forward! Follow onward roads,
The fire of Mays won't tire you out,
Among the endless line of moans
You'll feel again that new, new chaos.

You open your eyes and see – it's late,
You close your eyes – the skies won't flare.
Walk forward, you, no more a man,
The dawn at you will never glare.

What's happened to your soul, so kind,
Worn out now and rent in pieces?
It dreamed to stir the world with light,
You look at it and ne'er pity.

You shriek but nobody responds,
You meet the roads all empty, dull
In darkness shrouded and obscured.
Walk forward! Now it's late, it's done.

ლაშვარდ ცაზე დღეა თეთრი კრავების

ლაჟვარდ ცაზე დღეა თეთრი კრავების,
დასავლეთის კარი ჩატყდა ზმორებით;
უნაზესი ისმის ხმა საკრავების,
ბადებს იქით, სადღაც, გადაშორებით.
მზის გადასვლამ სივრცეები დაწმინდა,
იბინდება, იბინდება მთაწწმინდა.
აჰ, ეგ თმები, ჩემს სახეს რომ ეხება,
შუქმა კარგი მოგონებით შედება.
იყო ომი, იყო ცეცხლის დროება,
ლოდინია ეხლა და მყუდროება.
ციდან მთებზე ეშვებიან კრავები,
დაღალული წყდება ხმა საკრავების.

1925

THE AZURE SKIES ARE COVERED WITH WHITE LAMBS

The azure skies are covered with white lambs,
From lazy stretching Western doors collapsed,
The finest sounds of harps and pipes are heard
Away from gardens, where life's now at rest.
The setting sun has cleared the skies and clouds,
The late twilight is on the Holy Mount.[37]
Ah, hair of yours, that's touching now my face,
From light it's got the old remembrance paints,
There was a war, there were the fiery fights,
Now – cosiness and pending of new times.
The lambs descend from heaven to the mounts,
The weary sounds of harps and pipes die down.

ცელი კიჟის

ცელი კიჟის და ველები,
სურნელება დადგა თივით.
თივას თიბვენ მთიბველები,
ცა ლურჯია გუმბათივით.

დროს არ უყვარს დიდხანს დგომა
და ყვავილებს ართმევს დიბას,
მალე მოვა შემოდგომა
და ყველაფერს გადათიბავს.

1926

THE SCYTHE IS SCREAMING

The scythe is screaming in the fields,
You feel the flavour of haystacks,
Reapers are reaping hay in heaps,
Under blue skies, with breaking backs.

Time never loves to linger long,
Depriving flowers of fine silk,
Now autumn is to come so soon
To scythe all nature, everything.

ᲓᲐᲛᲔᲕ, ᲠᲐ ᲛᲝᲒᲘᲕᲘᲓᲐ?

ო, ყოველდღე მზეები
ქიმერებში ვარდება,
ქარავანი დღეების
მძიმედ მიემართება.
ის ოცნებაც ქაოსის
ნაპირამდე მივიდა,
დამეჳ, რა მოგივიდა?
ქარო, რა გემართება?

1927

WHAT'S HAPPENED TO YOU, THE NIGHT?

Upon the chimeras
Suns fall down every day,
A caravan of days
Is on its heavy way.
The dream that came from chaos
Is almost near its brim,
What's happened to you, the night?
Are you all right, the wind?

არც ერთ ეპოქას არ აქვს უფლება

არც ერთ ეპოქას არ აქვს უფლება
გაესაუბროს ჩემსას თამამად,
მას მომავალი ეალბულება
მხოლოდ გრიგალად, წვიმად, სამუმად.
გაუკვდავების ოცნებავ, მწირო,
გამვლელ-გამომვლელ წამთა ფერება
არ არის ეხლა შენთვის საჯირო —
რომ მოიპოვო ბედნიერება!

1927

MY EPOCH IS DIFFERENT

My Epoch is all different,
With it can compete no others,
Its coming days are surely meant
To cope with simoom and thunder.
Poor dream of getting immortal,
No need now to gain happiness
Through whiles and seconds that fondle,
Those passers-by, in merriment!

დღეთა კარებთან ვდგევარ წუხილით

დღეთა კარებთან ვდგევარ წუხილით,
ელვამ აანთო ცეცხლის ბუგრები,
ცა მემუქრება ჭექა-ქუხილით,
მე დამუნჯებით ცას ვემუქრები.

ელვამ აანთო ცეცხლის ბუგრები,
ხანჯლებს დავფარავ ისევ იებით,
მე მტერს იმავე ხმით ვემუქრები,
რომ მოვა ჩემთან მონანიებით.

1927

AT DOORS OF DAYS I STAND IN GRIEF

At doors of days I stand in grief,
The lightning has just lit the fire,
The claps of thunder threaten me,
I threaten heaven with mute lyre.

The lightning has just lit the fire,
With violets I shall cover swords,
I speak to foes still with my lyre:
You'll come to me with a remorse.

ვარდები

მე, ზამთრისაგან ჯაჭვაწყვეტილი,
ნაცნობ ბაღისკენ მივემართები,
სად ფერად უცხო, ყნოსვად კეთილი,
ზამთარ და ზაფხულ ჰყვავის ვარდები.

დე, ჰომიროსის და ჰესიოდეს
ფეთქდენენ ვარდები მადლა ახრილი,
მათ ვერ დამარხავს სასტიკი ლოდი,
სამუდამოდ ვარ ბორკილაყრილი.

დაე, მაისის ხატავდეს ხელი
ფლორას, გრაციებს, მუზებს და ეროსს.
რომელი იყო პოეტი წრფელი,
რომ სიყვარულზე არ დაემდეროს?

ვარდები იგი ელადის გემმა
დაფანტა, როგორც ძვირფასი ჩრდილი,
როგორც სახება და დიადემა
სილამაზისა და სინამდვილის.

რომელი ლხინი იყო უვარდო,
და ან – რომელი დღე საცნაური,
ან ანაკრეონს ვინ განუმარტოს,
რაა უვარდოდ დღესასწაული?

სახეთა ფერი და ნეტარება,
ბაგე, თითები თუ ყოფნა მზარდი,
პოეტს ყოველთვის აქვს შედარება:
მაისის ვარდი, სიცოცხლის ვარდი.

ROSES[38]

I'm unchained from winter's bondage
And pace towards a lovely park,
The whole year round there in foliage
Grow roses sweet and roses smart.

Let Hesiod's and Homer's roses
Never miss beats when rising up,
No stones can ever press them over,
I've cast the fetters off my harp!

Let hands of May draw wonder-pictures
Of muses, Eros, and of fleurs,
It's true, a poet sounds bewildered,
Who never speaks of love in words.

The ship of Hellas scattered roses
Like precious shadows, but all gone,
As if tiaras and the muses
Of life and beauty that are lost.

No feast has ever been created
Without a rose, each artist knows,
Anacreon, how could he make it,
A holy day without a rose?

Refined faces and blissful air,
The charm of being, that's rising high,
A poet can always find compare
For rose of May, for rose of life.

მარად იზრდება ვარდთან ჯინჯარი,
როგორც ოდესმე უთქვამს ოვიდის.
დაე, მოვარდეს სეტყვათა ღვარი,
და ცეცხლი ჩემზე გარდამოვიდეს.

ნეტავი ჩემთვის წუთებს არ ეკლოს,
აივნიდან რომ მესვრიან ვარდებს,
ვარდებს ეკლიანს, ვარდებს უეკლოს...
ოჰ, ამ დღეების სიმღერა მმართებს!

ო, სიწმინდეო და სიფაქიზე!
შენ ვერ მოასწარ, ისე დაწყნარდი,
როცა მზიანი იყავი ისე,
როგორც უწვიმარ რიჟრაჟში ვარდი.

და ორნამენტით აკრთობდა დემონს
იმ მშვენიერი წიგნების ჟალა,
წიგნთა ყოველთა მაშინდელთ ზემო
ვარდით მორთული ჩნდა თავის ქალა.

ბოტიჩელს ვარდთა სწვავდა დღე იგი,
რაფაელს იგი ფარავდა ლღინში,
სადაც ჯიოტო და ვან-დეიკი
და ლეონარდო იყო და-ვინჩი.

იხიბლებოდა სული დიადით,
როს სიმაღლეებს სწვდებოდა არსი.
რუსთაველს მარად შვენოდა ვარდი —
ისეთი ჰქონდა ვარდს შინაარსი.

With roses ever grows the nettle,
The poet Ovid used to say.
Let words in flows and torrents battle
With me alone, who burns at stake.

I hope those days have not run out,
In roses smothered when I stood,
Some were with thorns and some without...
I had to praise them as I could!

Oh, purity of tender skies!
You managed little, but soothed all,
You were so sunny and so bright,
As roses are at rainless dawns.

By ornaments was demon scared,
By those, embellish that books great,
Above the books a skull then glared,
Adorned with roses, all ornate.

Burned roses often Botticelli,
They cherished Raphael at least, –
Vandyke, Giotto and da Vinci
Were those who frequented the feasts.

The soul was charmed with all the great,
When essence used to reach sublime,
For Rustaveli[39] – a rose was main
Companion on the path of life.

ვიგონებ თაღებს, ვიგონებ სვეტებს
და ყვავილებით მოქარგულ ფარდებს,
მაისს, კოლხიდას, ძირფას პოეტებს
და კათედრასთან მიმოყრილ ვარდებს.

1927

Recalling pillars and huge arches,
And curtains in flowery design,
May, Colchis,[40] poets – dearest artists,
At rostrum roses thrown meanwhile.

გულო, რა გემართება?

შემოდგომის ყვავილებს
დიდებასთან მივიტან,
ერთი შორი ოცნება
მახსოვს ძველ მოტივიდან.
ვარდები არ არიან,
მაგრამ რა მევარდება?
სულო, რა გემართება?
გულო, რა მოგივიდა?

1927

IS LIFE TOO HARD FOR YOU, MY HEART?[41]

I'll carry flowers of the fall,
Fleurs fine, autumnal, to the Fame,
It seems I scarcely can recall
A dream remote of those past days.
No roses ever are around,
I hardly care for them, my love,
Why are you sad, my darkened soul?
Is life too hard for you, my heart?

* * *

აი, ფანჯარა იმ სახლის,
დაუვიწყარი ფანჯარა,
რომელთა დღეთა სიახლის
ჩემს გულში არა დარჩა რა.

სამუდმოდ ამიერიდან
დახურულია ის კარი,
საიდან მფენდა ნათელსა
ამომავალი ცისკარი.

გზებს მარტოობა ჰფენია,
ზღვას ხმა გოდებით დაღლია,
წინათ სასახლე მეგონა,
ეხლა უბრალო სახლია.

* * *

The window of that house,
The one I won't forget,
With it my joy passed bounds,
Though now it has all fled.

My luck has left for e'er,
For e'er is closed the door,
Through which I viewed with care
The morning star at dawn.

The roads are spread with malice,
The sea is tired of howls,
I took it for a palace,
But now – a mere house.

* * *

ქარი დასცხრა სიბობოქრის,
შავი ზღვიდან სიო მოქრის,
მე გიცქერი, როგორც ოქროს –
ჩამავალ მზეს, ჩამავალს...

მე გიცქერი, როგორც ქარვას,
შორითშორად ფიქრი ნარვალს,
თან გაატანს ქართა ქარვას,
ჩამავალ მზეს, ჩამავალს.

ო, ფიქრებო, მსევნო ტაძრად,
ო, ქცეულნო მტვრად და ნაცრად,
რად მიყვებით ასე მკაცრად
ჩამავალ მზეს, ჩამავალს.

* * *

The winds of storms have now died out,
The streaming breeze from seas still lasts,
I look at you as if at gold –
The big, declining, setting sun...

I look at you as if at amber,
As distant thoughts may look at ruts,
And whirling winds with hues of amber
Will follow hence the setting sun.

Oh, thoughts, that rest for long as temples!
What is left of you but mere dust?
You truly follow that ample,
The big declining setting sun?

* * *

მოდალატის ცხარე ტაში
და ორპირის ნუგეში
მეზიზღება, როგორც მაშინ,
როგორც სიჭაბუკეში!

* * *

A traitor's applause and loud cheers,
Consoling words, all false and queer,
Oh, I hate and disgust them now,
As I hated, when young, oh, how!

* * *

ქვეყანა გაცვდა, ვით ძველი გროში,
უდაბურებად იქცა სოფელი.
ნუ გაოცდები, რომ ასეთ დროში
მცირე ბედისაც ვარ მადლობელი.

შეიძლებოდა, მქონოდა სული
კეთილი, ნაზი, როგორც დობილი,
მაგრამ ცხოვრება არაა სრული,
მცირე ბედისაც ვარ კმაყოფილი.

ვით შეიძლება იქნე ლამაზი,
როცა სიტლანქე მოდის მგმობელი,
დროა, დაიტოვო ფიქრი ამაზე,
მცირე ბედისაც ვარ მადლობელი.

საშინელება, სიბნელე, გესლი,
დემონიური ცეცხლის პროფილი,
ბოროტო, სუნთქვა ნუ გამიაჩნელე,
მადლობელი ვარ, ვარ კმაყოფილი!

174

* * *

The world is worn out like a coin,
Now life is empty and quite dark,
Don't be surprised if at this point
I am grateful for a little luck.

I could have had a soul, as gentle
As is my kindest sister, but
Life's never so full and ample,
I'm satisfied with a little luck.

But how to be all nice and kind,
When clumsiness is attacking us,
It's time to leave the thoughts aside,
I am grateful for a little luck.

Horror, and malice, and even
Demonic profile of fire's cut,
Don't make me cease to breathe, you, Evil,
I'm grateful, satisfied so much!

* * *

სადაც შრიალებს ჯაობი ჭყვიშის,
შარასთან ორი ძველი ცაცხვია;
იქ ბევრი დარდის და ბევრი შიშის
გადამტან გულთა ფერფლი აწყვია.
ხსოვნაც არაა, გამქრალა ნიშიც;
რა სიმშვიდეა, რა სისაწყლეა!

* * *

The marshes rustle in vill Chkvishi,[42]
There on the road stand two old limes,
On grounds barren lay the ashes
Of hearts that suffered much in life.
Gone are their names, vanished are niches,
How bleak and bare now seems the life.

რა ცაა!

შეხედე, რა ცაა! –
ეს არის, რაცაა!

შეხედე, ამ მხარეს! –
ზღვით დილა გვახარებს!

შეხედე, რა ზღვაა!
ო, ეს ზღვა სულ სხვაა:

გულია, მიწაა!..
რა ცაა, რა ცაა!

1946

178

LOOK AT THE HEAVENS!

Look at the Heavens!
That's what happens!

Look at this clime! –
The morn seems kind!

Look at this sea!
Marvellous it feels.

The heart, the earth,
The skies are blessed!

ქებათა ქება ნიკორწმინდას

მაქვს მკერდს მიდებული
ქნარი, როგორც მინდა.
ჩემთვის დიდებული
სხივი გამობრწყინდა.
მკვიდრად ააშენა,
ვინაც ააშენა
და ციდ დაამშვენა
დიდი ნიკორწმინდა.

გზნებით დამკარგავი
გრძნეულ ჩუქურთმებით,
ქარგით დამქარგავი
ნაზი შუქურთმებით,
ნეტა ვინ აზიდა,
ან როგორ აზიდა,
რა ხელმა აზიდა
მაღლა ნიკორწმინდა!

რა განძი გვქონია,
რა მხნე, რა მდიდარი,
ჟდერს ქვის ჰარმონია —
დაროებს რამდი დარი.
კარგად გამოჰკვეთა,
ვინაც გამოჰკვეთა,
სიბრძნით გამოჰკვეთა
მძლავრი ნიკორწმინდა.

180

IN PRAISE OF NIKORTSMINDA[43]

I'm holding my lyre
As close as I wish,
A glamorous light
For me has been lit.
How solidly built
And adorned with skies,
Great Nikortsminda,
That rises so high.

Losing with passion,
So tenderly cut,
Embroidered with patterns,
With magic lace carved.
I wonder who raised,
And how did he raise?
What hands ever raised
Great Nikortsminda!

A treasure we own!
How bold and how rich,
Harmony through stone
Like songs we can reach.
Well cut! Oh, well cut!
By whom is it cut?
Great Nikortsminda
With wisdom is cut!

აქ რომ თაღებია,
სვეტთა შეკონება,
ისე ნაგებია,
სიზმრის გეგონება.
ნეტა ვინ ააგო,
რა ნიჭმა ააგო,
რა მადლმა ააგო
სვეტი — ნიკორწმინდა!

გრძნობ, ვით დიადია
თორმეტი სარკმელი,
ხაზებში ანთია
ცეცხლი მისარქმელი:
ნეტა ვინ აანთო,
რომ გრძნობით აანთო
და წლებს გადაანთო
ნათლად ნიკორწმინდა!

ხვეულთ დიადება
ვხედავ — რა უხვია,
დრომ მას დიადემა
კრძალვით შეუხვია.
ნეტა ვინ მოჰჭარგა,
და როცა მოჰჭარგა,
შიგ მიჰკარგა-მოჰკარგა
გზნება — ნიკორწმინდა!

The arches round here,
The pillars well tied,
They look as if come
From our dreams and skies.
I wonder, who built it,
A man of mercy?
A man of gift made
Great Nikortsminda!

You feel what is meant
By fire here in lines,
With twelve great casements
All burning till night.
Who lit the bright fire
For us to amaze,
Entrusting to years
Your beauty and fame!

The grandeur of twines
Is in abundance,
Time wrapped a tiara
In a gentle bondage.
But who embroidered?
And when embroidered
With passion in tints,
Great Nokortsminda?

მკვეთრი და მოქნილი
ხაზთა დასრულება
არის ამოდქმნილი
ნატვრის ასრულება.
ეს ის სიმკვეთრეა,
ეს ის სიმდიდრეა,
რაითაც მკვიდრია
ძეგლი ნიკორწმინდა.

შენის სულმნათისად
ასვლა ეროვანი:
ყელი გუმბათისა
მაღალღეროვანი,
ცამდის აღერილი,
ნებით აღერილი,
სათნოდ აღერილი
გშვენის, ნიკორწმინდა!

მზერა ქართულია
სივრცის დაუნჯებით,
თვალი გართულია
ფრთიან ფასკუნჯებით:
ფრთები, ფრთები გინდა
კიდევ ფრთები გვინდა,
გინდა დაეუფლო
სივრცეს, ნიკორწმინდა!

So sharp and so mild
Are ends of the lines –
It feels – a dream fine
Came true with man's mind.
It's due to the strength,
It's due to the wealth,
Great Nikortsminda
Is solid and firm.

Your rise to the skies –
The rise of the nation,
High neck of the dome –
What a creation!
It reaches the Heavens
And reaches with will,
It reaches with virtue,
With beauty to fill!

It looks with a gaze,
That is Georgian true,
With fire-birds are eyes
In mute space amused.
To conquer the space
You long for more wings,
Great Nikortsminda,
More wings we now need!

შენ, ფრთამოღუღუნეს
ქამთა სიმაღლეზე,
ჩვენი საუკუნე
გიცავს, უახლესი:
მძლავრი ხელოვნება,
ხალხის ხელოვნება —
ბრწყინავს საქართველოს
ქებად ნიკორწმინდა!

1947

A singer through wings
On the height of times,
Defended may feel
By hands of our time.
The power of the arts,
The art of our folk,
In praise of Georgia
Will shine evermore!

ნეტავ მალე მიაღწევდე მიზანს

შენ შუბლს იხსნი და სიბნელეს ლეწავ,
საქართველოს მოღრუბლული ზეცავ...
ნეტავ მალე აღმობრწყინდეს მნათი,
მალე სხივი მოეფინოს ნეტავ!

წინ მიიწევ და ხმაურობ, გღვიძავს,
საქართველოს სევდიანო მიწავ,
ნეტავ მალე დაამსხვრევდე ბორკილს,
ნეტავ მალე მიაღწევდე მიზანს!..

1954

188

AND GAIN YOUR DEAREST AIM

You show your face and break the dark,
You, Georgia's cloudy sky,
Rise blazing bright, I wish the sun
To make you full of light!

You are awake, you act, you move!
The land of sorrowed fame,
I hope you burst your fetters soon
And gain your dearest aim!

* * *

ყველაფერი
შეიძლება მოხდეს:
მთა მთას შეხვდეს,
მზე მთის იქით მოხვდეს,
ვარდი დაჭკნეს,
როს ბულბული მოსხლტეს, –
ყველაფერი
შეიძლება მოხდეს.

შეიძლება,
როს დაბნელდეს არე,
ხევებს იქით
გადაქანდეს მთვარე,
შეიცვალოს,
ვარსკვლავების არე, –
ყველაფერი
შეიძლება მოხდეს.

შეიძლება
შხამით სავსე სასმისს
გაწვდიდეს ხმა
მეგობართა რაზმის,
თან საშინელს
გიმზადებდეს რასმეს, –
ყველაფერი
შეიძლება მოხდეს.

190

* * *

Oh, anything,
Anything may happen:
The mounts may meet,
The sun will rise in challenge,
A rose will die
If nightingale loves heavens
And flies away –
Anything may happen.

It is possible,
If darkened are the skies,
Behind the trees
The moon leaps down, you find,
The stars won't shine
As bright as it happens, –
Oh, anything,
Anything may happen.

A group of men
That claim to be your friends,
May offer poison
When you're in a mess,
They'll rival you
All ruined you are unless, –
Oh, anything,
Anything may happen.

სამშობლოს წინ
ყოველ ვალთა მოხდის,
მშვიდობის წიგნს
გვირგვინს ვერვინ მოხდის,
მშვიდობის გზა
რომ ოდესმე მოკვდეს,
არა, ეს არ
შეიძლება მოხდეს.

1956

To do the duty
To the land, it means,
You truly love
The greatest Book of Peace,
The road of peace
Is ever blessed with Heaven, –
It never dies,
Oh, that will never happen.

* * *

რარიგ კარგია, სამშობლოვ,
შენი მტკვარი და რიონი,
შოთა, ილია, აკაკი,
   ვაჟა...

ორ ზღვათა შუა მდებარე
ბრწყინავდა კავკასიონი,
შოთა, ილია, აკაკი,
   ვაჟა...

სულ მაღლა გორის ციხეა,
სულ დაბლა ძველი სიონი,
შოთა, ილია, აკაკი,
   ვაჟა...

დააბლით კოლხიდის ველია,
მაღლიდან დგას ბახტრიონი,
შოთა, ილია, აკაკი,
   ვაჟა...

* * *

My native land, how sweet and dear
Are rivers Mtkvari and Rioni,
The poets: Shota, Ilya, Akaki,
    Vazha…[44]

Between two seas there brightly lighten
The mountains called Kavkasioni,[45]
The poets: Shota, Ilya, Akaki,
    Vazha...

High above stands Gori Fortress,[46]
Down here stands the old Sioni,[47]
The poets: Shota, Ilya, Akaki,
    Vazha...

The famous plane is of Kolkhida,[48]
The highlands are of Bakhtrioni,[49]
The poets: Shota, Ilya, Akaki,
    Vazha...

სადღეგრძელო იყოს მისი

ოცნებაო ჩემო ძველო,
ვართ ღამეთა მთევველი...
ბევრი, ბევრი სადღეგრძელო
დაგვრჩა დაუდევველი.
სადღეგრძელო იყოს მისი
ვინც ომებში იწოდა,
ვინც ირაკლის მარადისი
აღტაცება იცოდა:
მოდიოდა ერთზე ასი,
გზა გვუშვენოდა დიდების,
ჩვენ დავსცალოთ ყველამ თასი
ბედთან არ დარიდების!
სადღეგრძელო იყოს მისი,
ვინც შიშმა ვერ დახარა, –
ვიდგეთ ფეხზე... ჩვენ ტფილისი
ვადღეგრძელოთ ჯადარა!
აქ სიცოცხლე და ხალისი
ვის სხვად არ ესვენება –
სადღეგრძელო იყოს მისი
და დიდებით ხსენება!
ოცნებაო ჩემო ძველო,
ვართ ღამეთა მთევველი
კიდევ ბევრი სადღეგრძელო
დაგვრჩა დაუდევველი!

1958

LET US DRINK A TOAST[50]

O my oldest, oldest dream,
Sleepless nights you share with me...
Many toasts are left indeed
For the goblets to be filled.
Let us fill the bowls for those,
Who burned brave in fiery fights,
Who admired Irakli's[51] throne,
His devotion and his might.
Against a man a hundred rose,
But appeal to fame prevailed,
Let us fill the bowls for those,
Who fought boldly not to fail.
Let us fill the bowls for those,
Who stood tall and showed no fright –
We will rise in love and most
Of Tbilisi, old and bright.
Who loves life, enjoys it here,
Who is apt to merriment –
Let us drink for him, who's dear!
Indulging in enjoyment!
O my oldest, oldest dream,
Sleepless nights you share with me,
Many toasts are left indeed
For the goblets to be filled!

1. *Guria* – one of the western regions of Georgia.

2. *White cliffs* – Here the poet names three villages in Guria: Surebi, Dapnari and Nasakirali. The last is famous for white cliffs and woods.

3. *With Mary's Eyes* – Comparative study permits us to conclude that this poem is a free artistic translation of Lord Byron's *"Fragment"*, composed in 1805:

Fragment Written Shortly After The Marriage Of Miss Chaworth

Hills of Annesley, bleak and barren,
Where my thoughtless childhood stray'd,
How the northern tempests, warring,
Howl above thy tufted shade!
Now no more, the hours beguiling,
Former favourite haunts I see;
Now no more my Mary smiling
Makes ye seem a Heaven to me.

4. *Aspen Trees* – see "Translator's Introduction".

5. *Evening* – The poem was composed in 1915, when Galaktion was mainly absorbed in establishing the literary character of Mary. "Evening" proves to be a hymn to the Virgin Mary, namely to the wonder-working icon on Mount Athos.

6. *The Virgin of the Gate* – wonder-working icon of the Virgin Mary at Iveron, the Georgian Orthodox monastery

on Mount Athos. The Panagia Portaitissa (Παναγία Πορταΐτισσα, Greek for "Keeper of the Gate") or the Iveron Theotokos (Mother of God) is an Eastern Orthodox icon of the Virgin Mary. The original of this image is found in the Georgian Iviron monastery on Mount Athos in Greece, where it is believed to have been since the year 999. According to Eastern Orthodox tradition, this icon was painted by Luke the Evangelist. The icon is referred to as "wonder-working" because numerous miracles have been attributed to the intercession of the Theotokos by persons praying before it. It belongs to a family of images of the Theotokos known as Hodegetria (Greek: Ὁδηγήτρια, "she who shows the way") after the prototype from Constantinople. In these icons the Christ child sits on his mother's left arm and she is depicted pointing to Christ with her right hand. Another famous icon based upon Hodegetria is Our Lady of Częstochowa. A unique characteristic feature of this icon is a scar on the Virgin Mary's right cheek or her chin. A number of different traditions exist to explain this, but the most commonly held by Orthodox Christians is that the icon was stabbed by a soldier in Nicaea during the period of Byzantine iconoclasm under the Emperor Theophilus (829–842). According to the tradition, when the icon was stabbed, blood miraculously flowed out of the wound. The original icon in Iveron is encased in a chased riza of silver and gold covering almost all the image except the face, as is common with the most venerated icons. According to the Orthodox Church's sacred tradition the icon was at one time in the possession of a widow in Nicea. Not wanting the icon to be seized and destroyed by the iconoclasts, she spent all night in prayer and then cast the icon into the Mediterranean Sea. The widow's son later went to Mount Athos, where he became a monk and recounted the miracle of the bleeding wound, and how the icon had been placed in the sea. Much later (ca. 1004) the icon was recovered from the sea by a Georgian monk named Gabriel (later canonized a saint in the Orthodox Church) who was labouring at the Iveron Monastery on Mount Athos. This occurred on Tuesday of the Holy Week, and is commemorated annually on that day (as well as on the fixed date of March 31). The icon was taken to the katholikon (main church) of the monastery from which the icon gets its name. The tradition goes on to say that the following day, when the monks entered the church, they could not find the icon. After searching they discovered the icon hanging on the gates of the monastery. This occurrence was repeated several times, until St Gabriel reported that he had seen a vision of the Theotokos, wherein she revealed that she did not want her icon to be guarded by the monks, but rather intended it to be their Protectress. After this the icon was installed above the monastery gates, where it remains to this day. Because of this the icon came to be called Portaitissa or "Gate-keeper". This title was not new for the Virgin Mary, but comes from a verse of the Akathist to the Mother of God: "Rejoice, O Blessed Gate-keeper who opens the gates of Paradise to the righteous." Orthodox monks and nuns throughout the world often place the icon of the Theotokos Iverskaya on monastery gates. It is also common in Orthodox Church buildings to place the icon of the Theotokos Portaitissa on the inside of the iconostasis, above the holy doors facing the altar. There is a belief that this wonder-making icon may arrive in Iveron, i.e. Georgia, and when that happens the country will brighten up and flourish. Following this belief, due to the initiative of the Patriarch of Georgia, Ilia II, a new cathedral in the name of the icon is being built on Mount Makhata, in Tbilisi, to welcome it.

7. *David Narin* – King of Georgia (1225-1293),

distinguished for his faith.

8. *The sacred letters* – In the original text we have the word "ასომთავრული" (asomtavruli), meaning the ancient Georgian alphabet and texts composed in that alphabet.

9. *Shota Rustaveli* – see footnote 3 in "Translator's Introduction".

10. *Kaff* – In past centuries in English literature this word denoted the Caucasus.

11. *Mtatsminda* – მთაწმინდა, mount overlooking Tbilisi. In Georgian Mtatsminda means "holy mount".

12. *The riverside* – In the source text we have "მტკვარი" (Mtkvari), the river that runs through Tbilisi. It originates in Turkey (where it is called Kura) and flows through the broad valley of the Caucasus down into the Caspian Sea.

13. *The church* – In the source text we have "მეტეხი" (Metekhi), that is the church in Tbilisi overlooking the river Mtkvari.

14. *An old man's ghost* – According to the established tradition Galaktion here meant Akaki Tsereteli, a great Georgian poet (1840-1915) of noble origin, who deeply inspired him. In old age the poet was distinguished for his exceptionally gentle appearance.

15. *Daisy* – see "Translator's Introduction".

16. *The lonely bard* – In the source text we have "ბარათაშვილი" (Baratashvili). Nikoloz Baratashvili

201

(1817-1845), a great Georgian poet, great grandson of Irakli II, King of Georgia (see the note for the poem "Let Us Drink A Toast").

17. *Aspen trees* – see note 4.

18. *"Grave Digger"* – Galaktion's poem მესაფლავე ("Mesaplave").

19. *"The Night And I"* – Galaktion's poem მე და ღამე ("me da game").

20. *Anxious city* – Tbilisi.

21. *Sun of Ærraliða* – In the original text, for the month of June, the poet uses its ancient name "თიბათვე" (tibatve). Therefore, it is preferable to render it in English with a corresponding ancient word. According to the Anglo-Saxon Calendar June and July were together known as Liða, an Old English word meaning "mild" or "gentle", which referred to the period of warm, seasonable weather either side of Midsummer. To differentiate between the two, June was sometimes known as Ærraliða, or "before-mild", and July was Æfteraliða, or "after-mild"; in some years a "leap month" was added to the calendar at the height of the summer, which was Thriliða, or the "third-mild". (See: *A Month by Month Guide to the Anglo-Saxon Calendar* by Paul Anthony Jones, at www.mentalfloss.com.) The word *Ærraliða* must be pronounced with a stress on the second syllable – [aˈlɪðɑ:] or [əˈlɪðɑ:] as far as "ærra" (the same as modern "ere") here serves as a prefix.

22. *The Holy Grail, Grail* – the cup or bowl believed to have been used by Jesus Christ before he died, that became

a holy thing people wanted to find. See also "Translator's Introduction".

23. *Ol-ol* – pet name of the poet's first wife, Olga (Olya) Okujava.

24. On the poem "The Two Great Seas Have Met Each Other" see "Translator's Introduction".

25. *Mary* – In the original text there is "მერი ჩავორტი" ("Mary Chaworth").

26. *Towers of Grail* – word for word this fits the original Georgian version გრაალის კოშკები ("Towers of Grail"). The use of this word combination should be based on the following. Grail literature is divided into two classes: the first concerns King Arthur's knights' visiting the Grail castle or questing after the object; the second concerns the Grail history in the time of Joseph of Arimathea. Therefore, "the towers of Grail" denote "the Grail castle". On the Grail see also note 22, and the "Translator's Introduction".

27. *Lydia* – ancient Kingdom in Anatolia (7th-6th centuries BC), with its capital at Sardis. The last king of the Lydians, Croesus, was defeated by the Persians in 546 BC.

28. *Azure-Land As Rose In Sand* – The first word of the title of the poem "სილაჯვარდე" (silajvarde) means "azure", and is followed by "ანუ ვარდი სილაში" (anu vardi silashi), meaning "as rose in sand". If we replace the final Georgian words and say "სილაში ვარდი" (silashi vardi) instead of "ვარდი სილაში" (vardi silashi), which is permissible according to Georgian syntax, we thus get a new word combination homonymous to "სილაჯვარდე"

(silajvarde). That is why Galaktion puts between these two notions a conjunction, "ანუ", meaning "the same as" or "as", which in the Georgian language introduces equivalence. This way Galaktion creates a new enigma in which the Virgin Mary, as symbolized by a rose, is artistically depicted in the azure of the heavens.

29. *Shindisi* – a village near Tbilisi.

30. *A Rose In Sand* – In the original poem, as well as in its translated version, there is no mention of the word "sand" except in its title. This poem continues the theme touched upon in the poem "Azure-Land As Rose In Sand" (see note 28).

31. *She never knew a troubled being* – In the Georgian text we have a personal pronoun that corresponds to both masculine and feminine genders.

32. *Sun of Ærraliða* – see note 21.

33. *She died with somewhat helpless death* – Here "she" stands for the personal pronoun of the third person, "ის", which in Georgian implies both masculine and feminine genders. Galaktion associates the sun with the feminine gender, following the Georgian tradition in folklore as distinct from English, which leads me to render the Georgian pronoun with the English pronoun "she". A popular Georgian rhyme is the confirmation:

მზე დედაა ჩემი,
მთვარე – მამაჩემი,
და წვრილ-წვრილი ვარსკვლავები
და და ძმაა ჩემი.

204

The sun is my mother,
The moon is my dad,
Sisters and brothers
Are small stars ahead.

(My translation)

34. *Alazani* – river running in the East of Georgia.

35. *Faith* – In the original text we have "სვეტიცხოველი" (Svetitskhoveli), a cathedral in Mtskheta. In Georgian "sveti" means "pillar" and "tskhoveli" means "life-giving" or "living", hence the name of the cathedral. The history of the cathedral is based upon the following legend: according to Georgian hagiography, in the first century AD a Georgian Jew from Mtskheta named Elias was in Jerusalem when Jesus was crucified. Elias bought Jesus' robe from a Roman soldier at Golgotha and carried it with him to Georgia. Returning to his native city, he was met by his sister, Sidonia, who upon touching the robe died from the emotions caused by the sacred object. The robe could not be removed from her grasp and she was buried with it. The place where Sidonia is buried with Christ's robe is preserved in the Cathedral. Later, from her grave, grew an enormous cedar tree. St Nino, who preached Christianity in Georgia, ordered the cedar chopped down to build the church. She had seven columns made from it for the foundation, but the seventh column had magical properties and rose by itself into the air. It returned to earth after St Nino prayed the whole night. It was further said that from the magical seventh column a sacred liquid flowed that cured people of all diseases. The original church of Svetitskhoveli was built in the fourth century AD, during the reign of Mirian III of Kartli (Iberia). St Nino is said to have chosen the confluence of the Mtkvari (Kura) (see note

12) and Aragvi rivers as the place for the first Georgian Church. The present structure was completed in 1029 by the medieval Georgian architect Konstantine Arsukisdze (Arsakidze). It is currently the second largest church building in Georgia, after the Holy Trinity Cathedral, completed at the beginning of this century.

36. *Simoom or simoon* – hot dry violent dust-laden wind from Asian or African deserts.

37. *The Holy Mount* – მთაწმინდა (Mtatsminda), the mountain overlooking Tbilisi (see also note 11).

38. See more on roses in the "Translator's Introduction".

39. *Shota Rustaveli* – see the "Translator's Introduction".

40. *Colchis* – name given by ancient writers to the valley of the river Phasis (the modern Rion) in the west of Georgia. The Greeks regarded Colchis as the special domain of sorcery, a land of fabled wealth, as symbolised by the myth of the Argonauts and Medea.

41. For the scores of music composed for the poem "Is Life Too Hard For You, My Heart?" see the appendix.

42. *Chkvishi* – village in Western Georgia, where the poet was born.

43. *Nikortsminda* – ნიკორწმინდა, monument of Georgian architecture, a domed cathedral, erected between 1010 and 1014, which is dedicated to St Nicholas.

44. *The poets Shota, Ilya, Akaki, Vazha...* – Here Galaktion

names four major Georgian men of letters: Shota, Ilia, Akaki, Vazha, leaving the space for the fifth name blank. As has been acknowledged, under the blank the poet implies "და გალაკტიონი" – "and Galaktioni", as if inviting us to solve the riddle. In the Georgian language some proper names, when used without a surname, may have the ending "o" [i], like Galaktioni (but Galaktion Tabidze). Here the poet rhymes his name "Galaktioni" with every second line of each stanza. Therefore, in the translated version the Georgian form with the ending [i] is preserved to rhyme the name meant under the blank. *Shota* – Shota Rustaveli; *Ilya* – Ilya Chavchavadze (1837-1907), a great Georgian writer and public figure, inspirer and leader of the national liberation movement in the nineteenth century; *Akaki* – Akaki Tsereteli (see note 14); *Vazha* – Vazha Pshavela (1861-1915), a great Georgian poet distinguished for his deep understanding of the mysteries of nature.

45. *Kavkasioni* – კავკასიონი, Georgian name for the Caucasus.

46. *Gori Fortress* – historic fortification in the centre of the town of Gori, dating back to the tenth century BC, and reconstructed in 1774 by Erekle II, king of Georgia. *Gori* – ancient town in Kartli, Eastern Georgia.

47. *Sioni* – სიონი, Georgian Cathedral in Tbilisi, erected in the sixth century and restored at the end of eighteenth century.

48. *Kolkhida* – კოლხიდა, name dating back to the eighth century BC, given by Greek writers to the valley of the Phasis (now Rioni) in the west of Georgia (also known as

Colchis; see note 40).

49. *Bakhtrioni* – ბახტრიონი, fortress in Kakheti in Eastern Georgia, built by the Persians in the seventeenth century during their rule in this country. In 1659 the Georgians revolted against the Persians and destroyed the fort. The ruins still remain.

50. *Let Us Drink A Toast* – This translation is made according to a later version of the poem, the manuscript of which was presented to the translator by the poet's step-daughter (see "Acknowledgements").

51. *Irakli II* – ირაკლი *II*, the same as Erekle II, Georgian king (1720-1798), famous for his wisdom and courage.

APPENDIX
SCORE OF THE MUSIC TO GALAKTION'S POEM "IS LIFE TOO HARD FOR YOU, MY HEART?"
BY BIDZINA KVERNADZE

ბიძინა კვერნაძე

211

213